Two Little Devils

A Memoir by
Robert E. Holt

Exposition Press   *Hicksville, New York*

First Edition

© 1979 by Robert E. Holt

7-25-83

Library of Congress Catalog Card Number: 79-50193

ISBN 0-682-49362-7

Printed in the United States of America

To the memory of George Robert Bauer, who became as inseparably close as a brother, even when apart, and who brought years of great pleasure to my life

CONTENTS

TWO LITTLE DEVILS

BOB BAUER—BOB HOLT

To keep the record straight, we will call Bob Bauer "Big Bob" and Bob Holt "Little Bob."

Little Bob lived in his grandparents' house at 239 Brown Street in Grand Rapids, Michigan, with his mother and father and two aunts. Although middle class, they were considered quite wealthy at that time.

Big Bob lived with his parents and two older sisters at 235 Brown Street, Grand Rapids, Michigan.

Both three years old, Big Bob and I began playing together and even at this age Big Bob took the lead.

One morning Big Bob came over and called, "Hey Bob," and, upon hearing his voice, I went running to meet him. We then proceeded to scoot back and forth on the front porch. After a while we got tired of this and commenced pulling grandmother's flowers from the window boxes. When she saw this, she came through the front door yelling, "What are you two kids up to?" while at the same time grabbing for us so she could whack both of our hands. From then on we stayed out of her way as much as possible.

During that summer we both grew and were constantly together getting into all kinds of mischief. I distinctly remember getting into a quarrel with Big Bob over some bubble gum in grandmother's front yard. Big Bob, not too much taller than I was but always about ten to twenty pounds heavier, shuffled up to me and put up his fists, and we stood there looking at each other debating if we should hit each other or not. We both then cautiously backed away and Big Bob laughed and handed me the bubble gum.

The next three summers came and went, all filled with the

same kind of fun we had the year before, and with the fun came an even deeper and stronger bond between the two of us.

Finally it was the day when we both started school at the Buchanan School across the street from our homes. On our first morning, we entered school and took our seats along with the other children. We sat about three or four rows from the teacher's desk. Immediately, Big Bob spotted the teacher's bell and, while she wasn't looking, sneaked up to her desk and took it. He then nudged me, winked, and rang the bell. The teacher looked around and the other kids started laughing. She again turned away from us and ding, ding, ding went the bell. Then I took the bell from Big Bob and rang it again. At this point the teacher turned, grabbed her ruler and headed toward us. We both started down the aisle and ran around the room ringing the bell, ding-ding-a-ling, laughing and yelling with the teacher right behind us. Out into the hall and down the steps we went, running into the school yard where we promptly dropped the bell and took off yelling, "Teacher, teacher, we've got your bell." No need to say we didn't return to school that day.

We were still feeling frisky, and once we were sure the teacher wasn't hot on our trail, we decided to go into an alley where we knew we could pick some pears from a tree whose leaves and branches hung far over the owner's fence. The owner was a little old lady who, unfortunately, caught us and came out with her broom to chase us away. No pears that day, but there would be other days, we thought.

Walking down the street, I turned to Big Bob and said, "What do you think our folks will say?"

"Don't know, Little Bob, but we better get home by one o'clock."

"Okay," I said, "but first let's throw some stones and walk up to Burton Heights. Then we can go home." And that's just what we did.

Grandmother Holt was talking with Mrs. Bauer when we arrived, but she stopped to ask me how school was while Big Bob's mother questioned him. We told them it was fine. Everything was fine until 4:00 P.M., when, sure enough, that miserable teacher came over to tell everyone what we had done. After hearing what the teacher had to say, Big Bob's mother dragged him home where he was paddled. My paddling was administered on the spot by a very angry grandmother. We two boys went to bed very early that night.

From that time on, while we attended school, the things we did were a little less drastic than our first day—like pulling little girls' hair, or placing thumbtacks on the teacher's chair, or throwing the blackboard chalk at one another.

Big Bob didn't like school and would sometimes play hookey, but I tolerated it. Finally spring came and we were out. Hooray! We were ready for some more fun.

In the summer we rode our tricycles and played in our backyards most of the time. One day, while riding around, Big Bob said, "Hey, Little Bob, I've got three cents. Let's go to the grocery store."

"Okay! Let's go. Are you going to get me something, too?"

"Sure, Little Bob," he said. "Don't I always?"

Barker's grocery store, up the block and on the corner, was the old-fashioned type with a meat counter, shelves in the middle and along the walls, and jars full of stick candy, bubble gum, and pretzels.

"Say, Mr. Barker, what have you got for a penny?" Big Bob said.

"Well, boys, how about a pretzel stick—two for a penny?"

"Okay, give us two pretzels and some bubble gum, Mr. Barker. Here's three cents."

I quietly asked Big Bob where he got the three cents. He said he found them on his sister's dresser, and he was going to leave her a piece of bubble gum so she wouldn't snitch on him to his mother or dad. After we stuffed our pockets and mouths full of goodies, we decided to take our toy cars and run them in the sand.

That summer my parents decided to buy a house. They saw one they liked at the corner of Buchanan and Dickinson, two blocks from where we now lived. In that two story house were some really exciting things like a laundry chute from the kitchen to the garage below, with a pole like you would find in a fire-house. There was also a sloping driveway from the garage to the street which held great expectations for future fun.

After we moved in and got settled, Big Bob would bring over his wagon. We would place it on just the right spot in the driveway, run into the kitchen, climb into the laundry chute, slide down the pole, jump into the wagon, and go down the driveway like a bat out of hell.

All that summer Big Bob and I played firemen, sometimes to the dismay of my mother, and cowboys and Indians. We had a merry old time. My sister Shirley was born then. She was a cute little baby, but one I didn't always appreciate at the time.

But soon my father, who was in the real-estate business, began to feel the first pangs of the Depression. It was getting more and more difficult to keep the house running. At any rate, he got a chance to trade our house in the city for a ten-acre farm located between Coopersville and Marne, Michigan, about fifteen miles west of Grand Rapids, which he did.

When we moved to the farm, I was about seven years old and Shirley was about three years old. The farmhouse consisted of two bedrooms, a large living and dining room, a kitchen with a large pot-bellied stove near the porch, a basement with a dirt floor, and two small front porches. Outside was a toolshed, a chicken coop, a brooder house and barn, and, last but not least, a privy. We had no electricity or water inside; instead we used kerosene lamps and drew water from an outdoor pump.

2

THE DEPRESSION

By now the Depression had hit its peak and as far as business-men were concerned, many lost everything. My father lost every-thing but the farm and his Grand Rapids real-estate office. Being the proud man he was, he would not take charity from anyone. How he did it I will never know, but he kept his office going even though he never made a dime. He would stay in the city except for weekends. He eventually lost his old car too, so that when he did come home to see us, he would walk the fifteen miles to get there.

My mother had by this time gotten an old farmer to take eight acres of the farm land to work as his own. In return he plowed one acre of ground for a garden for us.

I started school at the Lillie School, a one-room farm schoolhouse, one mile down the old gravel road from our home.

The school itself consisted of mostly desks with benches, the teacher's desk, and a blackboard in the front of the room with a pot-bellied stove in the corner. There was also a cloak-room for our coats and boots. Outside we had two privies, one for the girls and one for the boys.

I walked both ways to and from school. I was then at the age where I could see by my clothes and what I had in my lunch bucket that I was the poorest boy in school. Most of the children were farmers' sons and daughters. They sometimes laughed at me and poked fun at my clothes and shoes. That was hard to take.

One afternoon after school, I went home and mentioned to my mother that the children at school were making fun of me. I had never told her of this before and probably shouldn't have then.

7

That night my mother swore that we would never sell the farm and that she would live to be far above anyone in the community. She was a proud woman, an educated woman, who was formerly a schoolteacher. Apparently, she had also been snubbed by some of the farm people. Actually my parents owned the farm for forty years before my father finally sold it on a contract basis, and in those forty years my parents became successful. They now live in a nine-room home and want for nothing.

It was becoming spring and I knew that after we got our garden in, I would go to my grandmother's for two or three weeks and would get to see my closest friend, Big Bob. I could hardly wait.

Finally June came, and I was sent to grandmother's. Without being told Big Bob knew I was there. We both had that same sense, it seems, of actually knowing when the other was close by.

In a matter of minutes after my arrival Big Bob was at grand-mother's door. Now we could go off together and I could tell him all about our living in the country and he could tell me about his recent experiences. He had been expelled from school a couple of days in early spring for too much horsing around. Otherwise everything was okay with him.

Grandmother didn't like to see us together. She always did say Big Bob was a bad influence on me and that he wouldn't amount to anything, but throughout the years this never once stopped our friendship. My grandfather was a big six-foot-two hulk of a man, and very handsome and jolly. He thought both of us boys were just "it."

The next day the circus came to town and set up its tents in the railroad yards about a mile away. Big Bob said he had a quarter and if I could get some money we could go to see it. Grandmother gave me fifteen cents and off we went.

On the way to the circus Big Bob said, "We're not going to pay to get in, Little Bob. Just follow me and I'll show you how it's done. We'll sneak in under the tent."

We looked around until we found a good spot. "Let's go in before the guard turns around and sees us," said Big Bob.

When we got in I said, "Look at all the animals. Here come the elephants and acrobats, let's get closer. Watch out, here come some horses and a riding show."

"Say, Little Bob, think we could get a job watering and walking the elephants?"

"I don't know, but let's try. I think that old, fat, bald-headed man over there is the one to see."

"Let's go and find out. Hey, mister, how about letting us water the elephants?"

"What's the matter with you two kids, you're too small for that kind of work," said the fat man.

"Oh yeah! Bet we could do it. How about it?" I said.

The fat man thought about it and then said, "Okay, you watch them while I go for something to eat. If you do it right, I'll give you a couple of tickets to the show." With that he left.

"Boy, Big Bob, this is something! Let's get that pail of water over there and give them something to drink."

We put the pail of water in front of them—the animals promptly put their trunks in the water and inhaled. Up into the air went their trunks—snort, snort, bellow, went the elephants and down came their trunks, all aimed in our direction. In a split second we were sprayed with water from head to toe. We just stood there, looking at each other. Finally, Big Bob said, "Okay you dumb animals, just for that we'll fix you. Get that pitchfork over there, Little Bob."

I knew immediately what was in Big Bob's mind. "I don't think we should do this," I said.

"Never mind what you think, I'm the boss, ain't I?"

I nodded my head yes.

"Well, bring it here," he said and so I did. "Now stand back and get ready to run like hell." With this, Big Bob took a running jump and sank the pitchfork right into the rear end of one of the elephants. The elephant let out one loud bellow, jerked so hard he pulled up the stake restraining him, and ran straight across the arena. He didn't stop when he came to the tent, but instead tore a hole through it and ran around in circles outside amongst the crowd scaring the hell out of everybody.

Meanwhile, we were just standing there watching all the commotion. "Let's get the hell out of here, Little Bob, here comes the animal keeper and guard. Run for the railroad tracks and home. But first we thought it would be fun to go up toward and across the open prairie, never once stopping until we got to an alley near our homes.

"Well, we made it. How do you feel, Little Bob?"

"I'm tired out. Let's rest a while. We still have all of our money and we saw some of the circus, but we better not go back. Let's swear now on our blood and honor that we won't tell anybody what we did today."

We both took the oath and then decided we had better go home. But first we thought it would be fun to go up towards Burton Heights and pound on the old lady's door and yell a little to see if she would come out to chase us.

The next day we overheard some grownups talking about an elephant getting loose at the circus, almost wrecking it besides frightening half the people to death. My grandmother asked me if I saw all that when I was there, and I said, "No, it must have happened after we left." That ended that.

During the next few days, Big Bob and I played cowboys and Indians in his backyard or my grandmother's backyard. Grandmother wasn't always too happy about this, since she had many flowers, as well as a nice rock garden behind the house, but we managed to stay out of her way.

Between the houses there was a stone and concrete wall. On my grandmother's side, between the wall and house, there was a width of about four feet so that we could jump from Big Bob's yard down into grandmother's yard. We would run, yelling and screaming, between the houses, out into the front yard, jump in our wagons, and tear off down the sidewalk at a tremendous speed. We would sometimes frighten to such an extent those people walking on the sidewalk, that they would jump into the street to get out of our way. We sometimes planned it so it would happen just that way.

Another of our favorite spots to play was in Big Bob's front yard. Underneath the porch was a crawl space about one-and-a-half-feet high. Around the edges it was boarded up, but, with a little effort, we managed to remove some of the boards and squeeze into the space.

"How do you like this for a good hideaway, Little Bob?"

"Pretty keen, but it's awfully dirty under here. Look at the ants and flies, probably have mice around too. Let's get some shovels and smooth the dirt so we can lie down in here," I said.

"Swell, we'll use this as our secret hideout."

We found a shovel in the basement, fixed the holes to suit us, and fixed the two boards we had to pull away from the side of the porch so that no one would know they had been tampered with. Then we went home to get our toy guns and caps, old shirts, and anything else that would make two little boys happy.

We would sometimes lay in our hideaway for hours, just talking and watching what was going on with the outside world. If anyone came near, we would be extra quiet so as not to be discovered. What we liked to do best was to sneak into the houses, steal all the fruit out of the fruit dishes on the porch or in the dining room, and quickly run back to our hideway. This would drive both grandmother and Bob's mother right crazy. I don't think they ever figured out how we could swipe the fruit and disappear so quickly without their being able to catch us.

Other times we would lie there and let our imaginations run away with us. Big Bob would claim to be Kit Carson or some other well-known cowboy, and I would be the Indian or the villain. We would conjure up whole regiments of soldiers and whole tribes of Indians—and they always fit under that little porch. Those days spent in our hideaway were some of the happiest days we both have known.

Along about my second week at grandmother's, Bob and I went under the porch, and, as we started to stretch out, I reached for an old shirt I kept there and out jumped a big grey mouse. It scared the hell out of both of us. "I'm leaving," I yelled, and out I went with Big Bob right behind me. The only trouble was he got his foot caught in the siding, and the more he pulled the tighter it held. By this time he was yelling at the top of his voice, "Hey, Little Bob, get me out of here before I'm eaten alive. There's more mice and rats in here."

I now had calmed down and came running back to help. I tugged and pulled, but to no avail. Then I had an idea. I would get the garden hose and water him down so he could squeeze himself out. When I told Bob of my plans he said, "Okay, just do it as quick as you can."

I went around to the back of the Bauer's house to get the

hose from the garage, hooked it up, and dragged it between the houses since the opening to the hideaway was on my grandmother's side. I turned on the water and aimed the hose in Big Bob's direction. Needless to say he got it right in the face. The water went all over, making the dirt muddy and, in turn, making him as dirty as could be—all the while he was yelling bloody murder and swearing at me like crazy.

At about this time my grandmother came running out to see what all the commotion was. When she saw Bob, she dashed over to get Big Bob's mother and they both came running back. Bob's mother was younger so she was the one who bent over and tried to pull his foot loose. Just then I opened up with the water hose again and got her right in the behind. She let out a yelp I thought could be heard around the world, at the same time calling me names.

This was too much for grandmother. She went into the house and called the police emergency squad. They came immediately and in about two minutes chopped a hole in the side of the porch and got my miserable friend out of his predicament. They finally left, but we didn't, even though we would have liked to. Both of us were marched to our homes, spanked, ordered to stay indoors, and told we couldn't see each other the rest of the day. This hurt us more than the spanking.

My father heard about the incident that evening, and since my father was a serious-type man, taking after my petite grandmother, he was ready to get after me. But my grandad just started laughing like crazy, picked me up, tossed me over his shoulder, took me out on the porch, and started to tell me stories. That was a nice ending to what I thought was going to be another spanking and I slept well that night.

It was my last week at grandmother's and I knew my dad's two sisters, Aunt Myrtle and Aunt Thelma, would want to take me shopping before I left. They both worked downtown in large, swanky stores and each year they would take me shopping and outfit me from head to toe. Sure enough, my Aunt Thelma, the persnickety one, awakened me in the morning, got me washed and dressed, and off we went in Aunt Thelma's boyfriend's jalopy; he was later to be my Uncle Ed.

They took me to Wurzburg's Department Store on Monroe Street where Aunt Thelma worked, and she bought me new shoes, a shirt, underwear, socks, a cap, and those damn knicker pants. I don't know why I had to wear knickers instead of long pants; my friend Big Bob always had long pants.

Aunt Myrtle, the jolly one, met us and I went with her to Woolworth's where we had something to eat topped off with a big chocolate sundae. Then she bought me some toys and finally, some clothes and a pair of long overalls, which are now known as "jeans." From there we went to my dad's office on the fourth floor of the old Whitcomb Building (I believe it ended up becoming the Kresge Building). To get to the fourth floor we either had to walk or ride in a creaky old "open" elevator. An open elevator was one surrounded on four sides by heavy screening and decorative brass work. We took the elevator. Finally it was time to go home for dinner.

It was along about this time that Big Bob and I made friends with several other boys in our neighborhood. There was Henry, the fat boy who lived next to Barker's Grocery Store, and was kind of a sissy, we thought; Neil, who lived four blocks away and was a big bully that we both had to fight at a later date; and Sonny, the Saint-Vitus-Dance Kid who lived one-half block from us on Brown Street.

My week at grandmother's was about over and, to my joy, my friend was going to come home to the country to spend a week with me. It was my Aunt Myrtle and her boyfriend Harvey, later to be my Uncle Harvey, who drove my dad, Big Bob, and me— along with a lot of groceries—home in Harvey's old touring car. When we got home, my mother greeted me as usual with hugs and kisses, which I'd just as soon wished she hadn't. By this time it was getting late in the day, and Harvey and Aunt Myrtle left for the city.

Big Bob and I got to sleep in the big bedroom that night, while my little sister Shirley slept in the other bedroom with my mother and dad.

3

BIG BOB'S FIRST DAYS ON THE FARM

We had gotten home from the city on a Friday night and I thought for sure my mother wouldn't make me go to catechism on Saturday morning, but I was wrong. By eight o'clock the next morning Big Bob, who was not a Catholic, and I were up. We washed and dressed, and were sent off to St. Mary's Church at Marne, to which we had to walk some three miles down the gravel road.

On the way, Big Bob asked me what catechism was, and I explained that the priest or one of the older people in the church comes out and talks to you about God, about being a good person, and about not swearing so you can someday go to heaven. I guess he accepted this explanation because he didn't say anything more about it. We met the three Swadlier boys on the way, and we all walked to church together.

St. Mary's was a small, frame, country church with a basement. On the main floor were pews, one main altar, two side altars, and the priest's room. The room opposite the priest's room was where the altar boys changed their clothes before serving mass. Along the walls of the church were the stations of the cross and at the rear or entrance to the church was a balcony where the organist and choir were located on Sunday mornings.

This Saturday, old Father Drew, many years with this church, a strict and stiff-as-starch type man, taught us our catechism. As soon as I saw him, I told Big Bob not to move or fool around, or surely the old man would send us to hell. The old priest looked around the room and spotted Bob. He asked him if he were a newcomer to the community.

"Yes," said Big Bob, "I'm from the city."

Father Drew said, "Well I'm glad to see you're a good Catholic."

"But I'm not a Catholic, I'm a Protestant," said Big Bob.

Old Father Drew looked at him for a moment and said, "Oh, you're protesting, eh? You mean you're a Protestant? Well, you just sit quietly and listen."

Our class went on for an hour, and then we all left.

On our way home we threw stones at the glass insulator bulbs that held the telephone wires to the cross pieces of the telephone poles. We must have been pretty good because we broke several of them. The Swadlier boys were teasing me about my knickers and Big Bob got so angry he beat up Georgie Swadlier. Then we simply went on our way.

Saturday afternoon and evening we roamed around through the cornfields and then went into the barn. We climbed up to the top beam, and jumped from there down into the haymow which we found to be good sport. Then we went into the house to dinner and bed.

On Sunday morning my mother got all dolled up and she, Bob, and I started to walk to mass. My father wouldn't go anymore. He had been a convert and old Father Drew one Sunday had brought up the subject of money in one of his sermons. He said it wasn't the old parishioners he had to worry about giving money, it was the new members that didn't give anything. Well, that did it for my dad. My mother tried to tell him that church was good, that it was just some people and some priests in the church that sometimes got smart, but it wasn't the church's fault. Dad wouldn't buy that! Many years later he went back to the church. Of all the churches I have been in, up to this day, the country church of St. Mary's still remains the most beautiful in my mind.

After mass we walked home and spent a very quiet Sunday afternoon.

On Monday morning my father got a ride into the city with a neighbor named Glen Cartiss, a man about my dad's age and a real good guy. Mr. Cartiss had three boys and later a fourth, not his own, but whom he raised as a son.

It was now strawberry picking time and I had a job on a neighboring farm picking berries for one cent a quart. I took Big Bob with me and the farmer gave him a job, too. Big Bob did not know a berry from a fly, so he did more damage to the strawberry plants than anything else. We got to throwing berries at each other and at some of the women in the field. Finally the farmer sent us home and told me I could come back but not to bring my friend. I didn't go back any more that week, even though I knew we needed the money. I wanted to spend as much time as possible with my friend.

About the fourth day of our driving my mother crazy, a friend of mine, Joe Browth, showed up, and after he became acquainted with Big Bob, we all left for the swimming hole which was two miles away at a creek called Sand Creek.

At the swimming hole, which was next to and under a bridge, and also full of turtles, crabs, and bloodsuckers, we took our clothes off and dove in and swam a little. We came out of the water and lay on the bank, taking turns picking bloodsuckers off each other. After a while, we put our clothes on and decided to go upstream where there was another swimming hole.

As we approached the second swimming hole, we heard girls' voices. "Hey, Big Bob, keep quiet," I said.

"Ya!" said Joe. "Here's where we have some fun."

We sneaked up to within a few yards of the swimming hole, where we saw four or five older girls swimming in the nude. We were old enough to enjoy the sight all right, and then we got the bright idea to steal their clothes. As we got closer, Big Bob grabbed a pair of panties from their stack of clothing, and began dancing around on the bank holding them in front of him and singing smartly, "Girls, girls, oh girls, see what I've got. If you want them back you will have to chase me."

The girls started to squeal and ducked under the water as far as they could, yelling at us all the time. Joe and I grabbed all of the rest of the clothes and we all three took off through the woods. We ran until we got back to the first swimming hole where we put their clothes, stretching them out on a big bush from one end to the other. Whether they found them there or not we never knew, nor did we care.

The next couple of days we spent roaming through the woods, climbing trees and running down cow paths, playing Indians and cowboys.

At Joe's house they had a lot of chickens, so we went in the chicken house, naturally, to get eggs. Big Bob found about a dozen and I found some too; then we began throwing eggs at Joe until he was covered. His mother saw us and came out and chased us away.

Just down the road near the train crossing was a little house turned into a small store. An old man we called Pete lived there and ran the store. This crossing was called the Titusville Crossing so we called the store the Titusville Store.

"Let's go to the Titusville Store, Big Bob, and upset old Pete."

"Okay, Little Bob, let's go!"

We walked into the store and there was old Pete sitting next to the corner stove. "Hi Pete, here's my friend, Big Bob."

"Hi," Pete said. "What are you up to?"

"Nothing," I said, "Just thought we would stop in to see you."

Pete was pretty smart. Rather than have us possibly lift something like an orange Nehi soft drink, he said, "If you two boys will go outside and wash my car (an old Model-T Ford pickup) I'll give you each a bottle of soft drink."

"Okay. Big Bob, let's go." We washed the truck in about five minutes flat, came back inside, sat around the corner pot-bellied stove, drank our pop, and listened to old Pete tell us stories of the days when he rode horseback out West and when he got shot.

"You want to see my wound?" he said.

"Ya, let us see it," said Big Bob.

Old Pete rolled up his left pant leg and sure enough there was a scar where he had been shot right above the knee.

"How'd you get it, Pete?"

He got red in the face and said he tried to take a cowboy's

woman in a saloon but since he had to leave in a hurry, that's what he left with. We finally decided we had better get home.

Walking home, Bob said, "Say, Little Bob, that tobacco-chewing Pete, he's some guy, isn't he?"

"Ya, Bob, but my mother doesn't like me to hang around the store, she says he's a dirty old man."

The week was about over and we were expecting Harvey to drive out from the city to take Big Bob home. We could hardly wait for Thanksgiving and Christmas to come.

4

SCHOOL AND HOME

It was time to return to the Lillie School when summer was over. At that point I was anxious to get back to school but wished it was in the city. However, I soon forgot about that since I had a lot of friends at Lillie.

On the way to school I stopped and picked up Joe Browth, and we walked there together. The first day was a pretty normal one. We were assigned our seats by Miss Jones, our teacher; at least I'll call her Miss Jones since I've forgotten her name even though she taught there for a couple of years.

After a week or so went by, we were in the swing of things and school became routine again.

It was late September and the evening when I returned home from school. It was the farmers' harvesttime and I helped my mother get in the potatoes, carrots, beets, and other vegetables from the garden.

During these fall days, mother was quite busy trying to get things ready for winter, and with taking care of my sister Shirley, my new baby brother Norald, and me, she had her hands full. Mother and I sometimes sat on the rear porch, which was nothing but a cement slab, and watched the sun set. She liked to tell me stories of when she was a girl, or to point out clouds in the western sky and say, "See there, Bob, can you make that cloud out? It looks like a dog or cat or an animal of some kind, doesn't it?" Sometimes the cloud formations looked like a series of buildings in the sky, something resembling a large city's skyline. We often talked about what we had to do the next day, or about school, but one thing for sure, mother always told me to be honest and not to steal, to keep my head about me at all times,

19

and if I was right, never to back down from an argument or disagreement. We talked about a good number of other things, like my dad, how hard the times were, and how much nicer the future would be once the Depression was over. We heard the sound of the train in the distance as it was going down the Grand Trunk Line, and we would wait for the sound of its whistle we knew would be blown as it passed the Titusville Store. My mother often wished she was taking a trip someplace on that train.

It was getting late into the evening now, and time to go inside. I pumped two or three buckets of water from the well so we would have water in the morning when we awakened. Mother went inside and lit a couple of kerosene lamps, as we had no electricity at that time. While she took care of my brother and sister, I started to read my books and do my homework.

The next day after school, Joe and I went up the road to an old farmhouse to get apples from the farmer who owned the farm. Old man Bushwell was always looking for cheap help with the work around the farm. After becoming acquainted with me, he found that I was a pretty good worker, and since I was a kid, he didn't have to pay me all that much. Anyway, I got a job for an hour after school, feeding and watering his chickens, geese and other animals, and sometimes getting the cows from the pasture to the barn. For this he gave me fifty cents a week and with that I would stop at the Titusville Store to buy a bag of oatmeal, or perhaps a few loaves of bread for the family. That about used it all.

One day we were all playing "ini-eye-over" in the schoolyard during lunch period. This is a game when, having chosen sides, one team moves to one side of the schoolhouse and throws a softball over the roof to the other side where someone catches it. Then the entire first team runs around the side of the building to try to catch the boy with the ball. If they do, they score one point. Anyway, during this particular lunch period I grabbed Harry Schabe thinking he had the ball. He was about a foot taller than I was, but I dragged him to the ground anyway.

"So you want to fight, eh?" he said.

"No, Harry, I just caught you," I said.

"Well, you little punk," he said, as he gave me a push which sent me sprawling.

"Okay," I said, and with that I got up and gave him a kick in the leg and the fight was on. All of the boys circled around us. "Crack him good, Harry," yelled one of Harry's friends, but Harry had a lesson coming to him. With my being a wiry kid, I wrestled, punched, and kicked, and ended up giving Harry a bloody nose. He picked himself up and went inside the school. I had no more trouble with Harry or anyone else in school from that time on.

That afternoon Miss Jones made both Harry and me stay after school for an extra half hour. We left together and Harry said to me, "Let's fix her!"

"How, Harry?"

"Well, Bob, I have a good idea. We're husking corn in the fields now and you know, every once in a while you find a field mouse in the corn. I'll capture one and put it in a small box and bring it with me to school tomorrow. You meet me before school starts, and we'll figure a way to put the mouse in Miss Jones's desk."

"Okay, Harry, see you in the morning." We then went our separate ways.

The next morning I met Harry in the schoolyard, and sure enough, inside his jacket pocket he had a little grey mouse. We fooled around outside for sometime and most of the boys got the word. I had the job of calling all the kids to school by ringing the school bell which was hooked to the top of the schoolhouse with a long rope attached.

When the kids heard the bell ringing, they started to go inside. We had it planned for Guy Peeche, one of my friends, to ask Miss Jones to help him with something or other, like seeing if the stove had enough wood and coal in it, at which time Harry and I sneaked up to her desk, opened the top sliding drawer, and popped in Mr. Mouse.

Miss Jones, now up in the front of the room, picked up some coloring paper from her desk and some first-grade readers. She distributed the coloring sets to the five or six kindergartners, and the first-grade readers to the next row of first graders. Then she went back to the blackboard and called the third graders and fourth graders up to the long bench, Harry and I included.

Miss Jones began by writing numbers on the blackboard for us to study, and then, going to her desk, she sat down and browsed through a math book. All this while we were waiting for her to open the desk drawer. She looked up from her book and said, "Bob Holt, what is two plus two?"

"Four, Miss Jones."

"Good, I see you have done your homework." I guess she needed a pencil or something, because she reached down and opened the middle drawer. Sure enough, out jumped Mr. Mouse, right into her lap. Miss Jones began screaming and yelling and doing a regular Irish jig right there between the blackboard and the benches we were sitting on. Mr. Mouse was running around like crazy and everyone in school began laughing—except all the girls who were getting up on their desks and yelling as loud as Miss Jones.

Harry and I just about burst a gut laughing, and so did some of the older boys. By now Miss Jones was racing for the door, and out into the schoolyard she went, still yelling. Meanwhile, we caught Mr. Mouse and turned him loose outside. It took about an hour before our teacher and everyone in the class settled down. It was probably good that this was her last year at the Lillie School. Who knows what might have happened! From that time on she was always leary about opening drawers, but she never did find out where the mouse came from.

It was Thanksgiving time. Uncle Harvey and Aunt Myrtle came to get mother, my sister, my baby brother, and me, to take us to grandmother's for Thanksgiving Day. Dad was still in the city and unable to get home in time to go with us. Instead, he went directly to grandmother's. Mother always managed to bring something to contribute to the holiday meal. This year it was three or four chickens which I had the pleasure of killing and plucking.

We had a wonderful Thanksgiving dinner around grandmother's big oak, circular table in the dining room with everyone laughing and joking and having a good time. When dinner was over, my friend Big Bob came to visit and, after he said hello to everyone, we both went out to play. We had lots of fun; there were many things to tell each other since it had been some time since we were together. The next day Harvey took us all home, but, before we left, I told Big Bob I would see him come Christmas and maybe at that time I would get to stay at grandmother's for a few days. He just looked at me and said, "Okay Bob, so long until then," and with that we pulled out of the driveway and started down the road toward home.

When we got back to the farm we unloaded my uncle's car; we had brought food and clothes from grandmother's and other things including an old, hand bottle-capper that came from who knows where.

My dad had acquired a taste for beer, home brewed as it was then. That afternoon, after Uncle Harvey had left, my dad found a couple of large old crocks in the cellar, each holding fifteen gallons or so, and, with beer hops, yeast, and some other concoctions, he filled the two crocks, put a cover on each of them, and went upstairs to tell my mother not to disturb them until he came home from the city again in about two weeks. He then left for Grand Rapids.

We had plenty of snow in the country, so much that the mailman used to come down the road with skis on the front of his car and tractor-like lugs on the rear wheels.

What I liked to do was to go to Coopersville with the farmer who lived on the hill and across the road to the north of us. Mr. Slaughter, a lawyer turned farmer, would hitch up his team of horses, stack his milk cans on a sleigh, and take them to the Pet Milk Creamery in Coopersville. Sometimes he would let me ride with him. The Depression had hit everyone by then— farmers were trading crops for cattle feed, women were trading or giving each other pies and cakes. Each helped the other as much as he could. It seemed a crisis makes most people think of others.

Glen Cartiss, who lived on the farm to the south of us, still had a job at the Marne Coal and Feed Mill, and I often thought he would have coal delivered to our house without getting paid because he and my father had become such good friends.

Each time I went down in our cellar it sure smelled from that home brew dad was making. I could hear it bubbling and I often wondered if it was going to explode. Although the two weeks had not passed, dad came home. It was the weekend before Christmas and sure enough he got out the old bottle-capper and he and I went into the cellar where he took the lids off the crocks to see if the home brew was ready for bottling. He took a hose he had borrowed from my mother's enema bag and siphoned the mixture into dark bottles. "Here Bob, hand me those bottles and give me a handful of caps." He filled the bottle, put it on the capper's base, put a cap in the top, and pressed down on the handle. Then he set the bottles up on a shelf, one by one. He did this all afternoon until he must have had 75 or 100 bottles capped. When we went upstairs he told my mother, "Don't open any of these." She just looked at him and smiled and went on doing what she was doing.

Soon Christmas Eve came and my dad was not yet home from the city. Finally I heard him come in the house about two or three in the morning, apparently half-frozen to death; he had walked the fifteen miles from the city, dragging a scrawny Christmas tree with him. Knowing he was home, I then fell fast asleep in my bed, which sometimes had snow on it in the morning because of a crack in the window.

The next morning when I awakened, I got up and went into the living room, and there was the tree, decorated with tinsel, candle lights, and some colored glass bulbs. Beneath the tree were a few things for us kids from grandmother, grandfather, and my aunts and uncles that were given to my mother at Thanksgiving time.

Sure enough, though, after we were all up and settled, my mother got me washed and dressed and off we went to St. Mary's Church, walking both ways, fighting snowdrifts, heavy winds, and falling snow. I thought this would be one day we would get out of going to church, but I was wrong.

I had made a few things for Christmas presents in our woodworking class at school and these were all I could give: my mother got a wooden cat she named Fifi; my dad a pair of handsome bookends; my sister a wooden doll. For my baby brother I had stuffed an old sock (clean) with things I thought he would enjoy. I had also made a few things of wood for my grandmother, grandfather, aunts and uncles. Needless to say, we had quite a few Christmases like this as I grew up.

One week had passed and dad thought the home brew was aged enough to drink, so he went down to the cellar and brought a bottle of it up to the kitchen, set it on the table, and opened it. It was so powerful that the beer shot up to the ceiling making quite a mess; he had about a third of a bottle left to drink. From then on he drank it in the cellar, probably because mother didn't like the idea of having to clean the ceiling every time dad had a bottle of beer, and probably because he could drown his feelings of sorrow about the Depression, off by himself where he wouldn't bother anyone. He got quite drunk that day.

The next day Harvey and Ed came to pick us up and take us to grandmother's. When we arrived, there was a large tree in the living room very beautifully decorated. My eyes almost popped out of my head as I looked around and saw a red sled standing in the corner, close to the tree. I didn't approach it or say anything about it since it might have been for someone else, but oh, how I was wishing it was for me. I just took my packages, such as they were, and laid them under the tree.

We then sat down for a dinner that seemed to be endless. Uncle Harvey, the fun guy, got up from the table and started passing around the presents, finally coming and giving me the red sled. I was out of the front door in two minutes flat, over to Big Bob's, and away we went, not getting back for two or three hours. We both returned sloppy wet from falling off the sled and rolling in the snow. By this time they all had opened their presents and grandmother called me over to tell me how much she appreciated and liked her little "Fifi." I had made grandmother the same kind of wooden cat I had made for my mother. For years to come it remained on the buffet in her dining room, where it was seen by all.

It was during the Christmas holiday that my sister Shirley

was looking through some magazines with pictures of babies in them when she suddenly blurted out, "Look what they call babies, Zimbo's." It was really Bimbo's, but she couldn't pronounce her "B's." When my mother and the rest read it, they all started calling Norald, my brother, Bimbo. To this day he is called "Bim" by the family and all those who have known him for years.

That evening the family left for home, but I stayed at my grandparents for the rest of the week. Bright and early that first morning Big Bob showed up with two pairs of clamp-on skates. We had some cereal with bananas for breakfast and then I put on my hightops, which were a Christmas present, and off we went down to the pond near the railroad yards.

When we got to the pond, Big Bob said, "Little Bob, go over to those trees and get some branches and wood and we'll make a fire."

"Okay," I said, and did as he told me, but we couldn't get a fire going.

We both thought for awhile and then Big Bob said, "I know what we can do! Follow me, but stay down. We'll get some oil rags from the boxcars to light our fire."

Now for those of you who don't know anything about boxcars let me explain to you about the railroad's use of oil rags. Under the boxcars near the wheels were little metal boxes with oil-soaked rags to lubricate the wheels of the train so they wouldn't make a screeching noise as they went down the track.

Well, we sneaked around the boxcars stuffing our pockets full of the rags as we found them, all the time keeping an eye out for the yardmen so that they wouldn't catch us. We made it without being caught and then came back to start our fire. What a fire that was! It must have shot twenty-five feet into the air, singeing our stocking caps and hair as it went up.

"Some fire, eh, Little Bob?"

"Yeah, now we can keep plenty warm," I said.

About this time along came Fatso Henry and Sonny, the Sun-Dance Kid. "Hi! you guys," said Fatso.

"Hi, Fatso, Sun Dance, how do you like our bonfire?"

"It's great, Big Bob, how did you get it to be so big?"

"Can't tell you that. It's Bob's and my secret. Say what are you chewing Fatso? What have you got there? Let's see!"

With that Big Bob turned to me and said, "Grab his feet, Little Bob," so I tackled Fatso and started grabbing at his pockets as we rolled around on the ground. Sure enough he had some hard candy canes in his pocket, which we took.

"Now you can skate, Fatso and get warm by our fire," I said.

Then Big Bob said, "Thanks for the candy, Fatso, and if you tell your mother, I'll beat you up."

We had forgotten about the Sun Dance kid until now and I said, "Hey, Big Bob, what about Sun Dance?"

He looked at Sun Dance and said, "Leave him alone, don't get him excited or he'll jig right through the bonfire."

Our spot was now starting to get crowded; Neil, the bully, and his crowd came along. Right away he thought our bonfire wasn't any good. The only way it would have been any good was if he had made it.

"Big Bob," said Neil, "your little friend is a jackass," meaning me.

"Oh yeah!" said Big Bob. With that he whopped Neil smack in the face and they went to it hot and heavy, both being up and down several times.

"Have you had enough, Neil?" asked Big Bob.

"Yes, but I could beat your friend if you would stay out of it," said Neil.

"Oh yeah, try it," I said.

Big Bob turned to me and said, "Forget it, he's too big for you."

This made me even more angry. "The hell you say, Big Bob, I'll whip him and you stay out of it."

He laughed and said, "Okay, go to it."

I looked at Neil. "Okay Neil, any time."

Well, we got to fighting and somehow I got the best of Neil, knocking him right into the fire. He came out of there yelling he had enough. After rolling himself around in the snow to make sure he wasn't on fire, he looked at me and said, "You're okay Bob, let's be friends." From then on we all got along fine.

When I got home my grandmother really gave it to me. My jacket was ripped, I had lost my mittens, my cap was burned, not to mention my singed hair and eyebrows, and I felt miserable. I was yet to learn what kerosene and sugar, and molasses and sulphur were for.

The next morning I was sick with a cold, not to mention a bruised cheekbone and sore ribs. Grandmother rubbed me down with something that felt as hot as that bonfire we started the day before. Then she took a tablespoon of half kerosene and half sugar and made me swallow it. I thought my insides would burn up. A little later she came with a cup of molasses and sulphur; after about four spoonfuls of this I must have turned yellow because she ran to the bathroom to get a wet towel to put on my forehead.

Later that afternoon, not only did grandmother give me more kerosene and sugar, but she found some of grandfather's old glass tubes that lit up with a bluish glow and made a funny sizzling noise, when plugged in, and she rubbed them over my back, arms, legs, and chest. I thought for sure she was going to electrocute me, but surprisingly enough, when she finished I felt pretty good. I was in bed for a couple of days and this ended my vacation for that Christmas. Big Bob and I said goodbye and I left for home once again.

5

MICHIGAN WINTERS

It was January of 1932, and my dad and a few friends from Grand Rapids came home for the weekend. These were Prohibition times and if anyone had any alcoholic beverage it would be either bootlegged or home brew. Along with dad came Big Dutch the bootlegger, Sam the policeman, Jim Frye, a bald-headed Irishman, and all their girl friends, pulling up in Big Dutch's Buick sedan, and bringing a big snowstorm with them.

As they came in, they all brought packages of food, plenty of bootleg whiskey, "hootch" as Dutch called it, and popcorn and candy for us kids. Dad introduced Big Dutch and his girl friend, Liz, to my mother; she already knew Sam, Jim, and their girl friends.

It was good that they brought food with them because we were all snowbound for three days and no one could get out or in except to beat a path to the outside privy.

Jim was a merry old Irishman who could sing and tell stories like a professional entertainer. He must have liked kids because he sure had fun with my sister, brother, and me, and he never failed to bring us something in the few years he visited with us.

After having something to eat that night, I went to bed but didn't sleep; I wanted to hear what was going on in the living room.

My dad went down to the cellar and came up with his beer, which they all sampled, and then Big Dutch opened a bottle of his "hootch."

"I got me protection along," Dutch said to the others. "Good old Sam. Say Sam, show them your badge and gun."

I guess he did, but anyway, Sam said to my father, "Rex, go put this hardware someplace where no one knows where it is."

By now my mother, who could play any song on the piano by ear, was belting out some fast music, including "Hail, Hail, The Gang's All Here." How they were all able to see I don't know, because all we had were five kerosene lamps but I guessed they weren't concerned with seeing, only having fun. Peeking through a crack in my bedroom door, I saw Jim singing like mad, Sam dancing with his swinging girl friend, and Big Dutch in the corner chair with Liz on his lap, necking and saying, "Liz baby, be a good girl." This must have gone on for hours but I finally fell asleep. When I got up about noon the next day, everyone was stretched out all over the place, on the couch and in the chairs, except for Big Dutch who was lying on the floor.

My mother put a mammoth kettle of water on the stove, and threw in onions, beets, potatoes, turnips, some ham hocks and salt and pepper. This cooked for about three hours, giving off a lot of steam, as well as smelling up the place. She called it her Irish stew or boiled dinner. Everyone ate, but how they kept it down I don't know. It couldn't have been as bad as I thought it was, as they had this for another couple of days, and everyone survived.

On the third day the storm lifted. Dutch, my dad, Sam and Jim pushed open the front door and shoveled a path to Dutch's car which was buried up to the roof; we had had four to six feet of snow. Later in the morning the country snowplow came along, using another plow behind it for more power, and opened up the country road to the main highway at Titusville.

Meanwhile, Jim and my dad walked up the road to a farmer's house to ask him if they could use his horse to pull Dutch's car out of the snow. They came home and shortly thereafter the farmer came with a team of horses. Big Dutch and Sam now had a few more drinks and Dutch went outside.

The farmer approached him and said something that really angered him. Dutch reached inside his Buick and pulled out a billy club which he promptly swung around as he circled the farmer.

"Get this damn car out into the road before it snows again," Big Dutch said. Needless to say, that car was put in the road in about three minutes flat. "Here you old goat, here's a bottle of twenty-five-dollar hootch for your trouble. Now get the hell out of here."

Into the car climbed Dutch and Liz, Sam, Jim, and their girl friends, and off they went, promising to be back next month.

Now the latter part of January, we were getting one snow storm after the other. My mother said she thought we got the snow from Canada and the Western Plains across Lake Michigan as that part of Michigan was a real snow belt.

I had caught my second cold that winter and that was one of the worst things to do in our house. Mother used my grand-mother's remedy of kerosene and sugar, plus a few of her own remedies. I got up in the morning, put some coal and wood in the pot-bellied stove, washed my face, hands, and arms in a pan of almost ice water, and took a fork and toasted a couple of slices of bread over the stove's hot coals. If you have never had bread toasted over hot coals you don't know what you're missing —there's nothing like it.

My mother, after giving me a teaspoon full of kerosene and sugar, took some smelly grease, lathered it on my neck and chest, put a wool sweater on me for warmth, and worst of all, wrapped a dirty old sock around my neck. "It has to be dirty to be effective," said my mother. Then she bundled me up with an old jacket and mittens, handed me my lunch, and off I went to school.

On the way I met some of my pals. Further down the road we picked up Joe Browth who immediately spotted the sock around my neck.

"Say Bob, what have you around your neck?"

"Yeah," said Harry and Fred, "let's see."

"Nothing," I said, "and anyway, it's none of your business." Before we got to school we managed to throw a few snowballs and get pretty messy from the snow. I had by this time gotten rid of the dirty sock.

That semester I sat at a desk next to Carroll Van Otter, with

Betty Poplar on the other side of me. Betty liked me and I liked her, but this day she kept turning her head away and sniffing.

Finally Carroll looked at me and said right out loud, "You sure stink Bob Holt, what have you got on?"

"None of your business Carroll, and I'll punch you in the nose if you say that again."

Miss Jones came down the aisle to my desk to find out what the disturbance was. When I told her my mother had greased me up because I had a cold, she laughed and told the other kids not to tease me. What had happened was that the heat in the school was making the grease smell, and wearing that old wool shirt wasn't helping matters either. Anyway, after a few days I was over my cold and more acceptable to my classmates.

The following week in late January, I again started the week off by walking that mile to school through snowdrifts and a blinding snowstorm. I rang the school bell and went inside. I saw that only about two thirds of the class came to school, amounting to some twenty to twenty-five kids. We stayed indoors during our lunch hour as a real blizzard developed.

Along about 2:30 P.M. old man Bushwell came to the school looking like he had been through a mountain of snow and ice. He told our teacher that everyone around was snowbound and to count all of us children, bundle us up, and wait until Farmer Buickemeyer from across the road from Bushwell's farm came with his milk wagon and team of horses. Then Bushwell would take some of the children to his house, and Buickemeyer would take Miss Jones and the rest of the children to the Buickemeyer house to stay the night. Farmers Bushwell and Buickemeyer lived about two city blocks from the school, but it took Mr. Buickemeyer and his team of horses almost thirty minutes to reach the schoolhouse.

As children, we were all excited and looked forward to being snowbound and not being able to get home. We didn't even think of our parents and how they would learn about us as most of the telephones were not working. It wasn't until later that night that we realized how serious a snowstorm could be.

When we finally got to Buickemeyer's farm, half of the kids

went across the road to old Bushwell's farm and half went in the house with Mr. Buickemeyer. I started across the road when I heard farmer Bushwell call, "Bobby." That's what he called me even after I grew up. "Come with me, you're staying at my place," he said.

"Okay, Mr. Bushwell," I said respectfully, and tagged along after him.

After several of us were situated in the Bushwell farmhouse, the old man went across the road to Buickemeyer's to see what they could do about letting our parents know where we were. Finally he came back. They had been able to reach some of the homes by telephone, but only in the southerly direction from school, which meant those parents living in the northerly direction wouldn't know where their children were. The telephones we had in those days were the old crank kind, and I couldn't figure out how any messages could get over those boxes anyway.

Some of the girls were put up in beds, but for the most part we slept in chairs or on the floor. Later that night I began to worry a little, but then two men came to the door to say they were trying to get to the houses of those parents who weren't already contacted, or to houses as near as possible so that others could tell the parents we were all safe and sound. I finally fell asleep.

Early the next morning I awoke to see a young man half-frozen to death sitting in the kitchen next to Bushwell's old iron cooking stove. He was drinking cup after cup of coffee and babbling that he had been out all night, was lost three times, but had gotten through to most of the children's homes to the north of school. The young man had frostbitten feet and hands by that time and Bushwell was rubbing snow on them to bring back the circulation. We all had a sense of relief and thought we would be going to either school or home the next morning, not knowing we would be snowbound for another day and night.

Poor old Bushwell. Joe, Carroll, Guy, Dan Peecher, and I decided to go to the barn to help out with the chores. We had a hilarious time. The cows kicked when we tried to milk them; when we cleaned the gutters of dung behind the cows, we threw the dung in the walkway where we all ended up stepping in it; and when the cows were milked, we knocked the whole milk can over. Old man Bushwell was swearing like a trooper. He told us to make our way back to the house and stay the hell out of his barn. Our good deed didn't turn out too well.

It was good that we were on a farm because Mrs. Bushwell made a lot of homemade bread and soup to feed our hungry group.

Old man Bushwell was relieved when the storm lifted and all of us kids went our merry way. When Shirley and I got home, mother couldn't stop hugging us, which bored me and delighted Shirley. But we were home and there would be no more school that week, which made all the hugs and kisses worthwhile.

Later that week double snowplows came through and opened up the roads. The grown-ups said that some of the chunks of snow the plows threw off the roads as they came through weighed as much as three hundred pounds!!!

After getting home from church on Sunday, I put on my old clothes, picked up my clamp-on skates, and asked my mother if I could go skating. "Yes, Bob, but be home before dark," she said, and off I went.

I went to the Browth farm and picked up Joe. We then went to the woods, put on our skates, and skated down the frozen creek for approximately a half mile to a thick swampy pond encircled with trees and brush. Joe and I raced each other across the pond, tried to make figure eights, and dashed in and out of the heavy brush that grew right up out of the water. Later that afternoon we returned to Joe's house and had popcorn and some cookies, and with the day being over, I returned home.

The rest of January was bitter cold. Sometimes snow fell, and yet other days the air was crystal clear with bright and sunny skies.

In February we had more snow, and my birthday. My father managed to get home on the weekend. I remember he came into our bedroom early in the morning when I was just waking up.

"Happy Birthday, Bob—I have something for you," and he gave me a red yo-yo. I was thrilled to death, cried, took the yo-yo, and hugged my dad. My father's expression was one of a deep love for his son. He didn't say anything but turned and walked out of the room. Dad always was a quiet man who found it difficult to show his emotions. It was the best present I have ever received in my life for the simple reason that I knew my dad had sacrificed something to buy me a five- or ten-cent yo-yo during times of hardship.

My dad had started back to the city without filling the wood box and we were running low on both wood and coal for the stove. Mother decided to go up the road to Farmer James to ask if we could take brush and old logs that were in his woods and pastureland which bordered our farm at the southwest corner. Being a nice old fellow, Mr. James said we could have all that we wanted. My mother, being a proud woman, waited until nightfall; then she bundled me up and we went looking for wood. I trudged along through the field with her, climbed the fence between our properties, and walked through the pasture to the edge of the woods. Mother found two or three logs, actually they were old fence posts, and tied one end of them together so they could be dragged easily, while I picked up small branches and sticks. We dragged the logs home and put them in the back room along with the sticks and branches.

We made three trips that night, and for the balance of the winter made three trips every four nights. Mother and I sawed the logs, using an old rusty saw we had in the cellar. With some coal we already had, and the wood we gathered, we were able to get through the balance of the winter.

Toward the end of February, true to his word, Big Dutch and his gang, Sam, Jim, and their girl friends, showed up on the door-step for a weekend of hilarious fun, which meant more boiled dinners, "hootch," home brew, many songs, and much noise. The time passed so rapidly it seemed as if they had just gotten there and were already leaving.

March came in like a lion, windy and snowy, with many ice storms. Some days I could hardly make it to school. Finally, around the middle of March, it was maple syrup time which meant I could go to Guy Peecher's for one day and one night. On Thursday Guy asked me to ask my mother if I could stay at his house Friday night and Saturday, as his dad was now harvesting and making maple sugar syrup. Mother said yes.

The next morning I met Guy on the road to school.

"Hi Guy, I can go to your house today after school."

"Swell, Bob," he said and we continued on toward school, running and horsing around along the way.

When school was over we walked the mile and a half to Guy's house. Then we walked to the woods where Guy's dad was just bringing the snow sled and horses from the other side of the woods to the wood shack where he poured the buckets of maple sap he had collected into long metal pans. These metal pans were heated from a fire underneath, and the maple sap boiled and ran in long metal troughs similar to rain gutters, to another metal pan, and then through more troughs set in cold water to cool the maple sap. At this point the sap could be drunk. Finally, it went on to the last metal pan where the syrup was entirely cooled and bottled or put in candy trays to harden.

"Here, Bob, take a cup of maple sap, it's good."

"Okay, Guy. Say, that is good. Let's have some more."

"Okay, Bob," said Guy, and we took our metal cups to the other end of the shack out of sight of Guy's dad and proceeded to drink four or five cups of the stuff.

That night after supper, Guy and I went upstairs to bed and all of a sudden the maple sap we had drunk started working on us, and we both were making beelines to and from the outside privy for about two hours straight.

The next morning was a busy one. We were up early, went to the barn and helped with some chores, and then had our breakfast. Guy and his brother Don, Mr. Peecher, and I left for the woods on the snowsled to gather more maple sap.

At the shack Mr. Peecher said, "Don, you think you can drive the horses and sled and make the run through the woods, pick the buckets off the maple trees, and get the sap back here while I start the fires and get things in order?"

"Sure Dad," said Don.

"All right, then take Guy and Bob with you."

Off we went through the woods with Don driving the team of horses.

"Giddiup there—whoa," said Don to the horses. "Okay, you and Bob go fetch those two buckets from those trees over there and put these two empty buckets in their place. And be careful not to spill any of the sap." This kept up for about an hour and we now had collected about fifty buckets of sap in the sled.

"Guy, you and Bob go down over there and bring back those four buckets of sap."

"I'm tired, go get them yourself," said Guy to his brother.

Don just looked at him and then said, "Bob, you go get them."

"I'm tired, too, why don't you get them? All you've done is sit and drive the horses."

"If you and Guy will get those last four buckets of sap I'll let you both drive the horses part way back to the maple shack," said Don.

That really sounded exciting, so Guy said, "Okay Don."

We collected the last buckets in a hurry, got in the sled, and sat on the seat behind the horses. Don passed the reins to Guy who yelled giddiup to the horses. On our way through the woods Guy slapped the horses with the reins and they bolted and took off with all of us holding onto our seats for dear life, and with maple sap spilling and flying every whichway. We were all yelling "Whoa, whoa" for the horses to stop, but they kept racing through the woods, across the small creek, and then finally stopped a little way from the wood shack.

We all had maple sap on us from head to toe. Mr. Peecher heard us coming and came running out of the shack, tied the horses, took one look at us and the wagon and yelled, "You kids get the hell out of here and go home. You've ruined half a load of maple sap."

We left as fast as possible. Mrs. Peecher washed all three of us the best she could; then I started for home, my hair and clothes still sticky from the maple sap.

At first, because I was pretty well covered with snow, my mother didn't notice the condition I was in.

"Did you have a good time, Bob?"

"Yes, Mom, but I don't know if I'll go back to Guy's during maple syrup time next year," I said.

By now my clothes were drying out a little, then Mom saw how sticky they were, and did I catch hell. She heated water, poured it in our galvanized tub in the back room and scrubbed me until I thought my skin would peel off. Then she put me to bed with a stiff reprimanding.

March was just about over and the snow was melting fast. It would soon be Easter Sunday and spring in all its glory would arrive.

6

EASTER AND SPRING

In our part of Michigan, as I remember, April usually came in with a high and bright sun, cool crisp mornings, warmer days with robins singing and daffodils, tulips and many other flowers showing their faces, and all of nature breaking through the earth to bloom to announce spring is here and summer is on its way. As a boy, and even to this day, I've felt that wonderful feeling of being born again during that beautiful season called spring.

We still had a few chickens which we had managed to keep alive during the winter months, and with Easter almost upon us, my mother started preparing different things for the holiday as best she could. I gathered the eggs and mom would hard-boil them. We children would then use crayons to color them. I knew my dad would be home for Easter. He never missed spending the holidays with us no matter what it took to get home.

Easter that year was on a bright and clear, but quite crisp day. Mother, Bim, Shirley, and I started out for eight-o'clock mass at St. Mary's Church in Marne. We walked part of the way and got a ride about a mile from home with the Schwaldier family. The church was filled with people, and the altar had been decorated with flowers. The little country church was very beautiful, a place where you could feel at peace with yourself and everyone in the world.

The old priest of many years had passed away and St. Mary's now had a new priest by the name of Nugent, a very small man in stature who was a very humble and religious person.

After Easter services the next mass was at ten A.M., so my mother took me to see Father Nugent to ask if she could enter me as an altar boy. I didn't mind this, but I knew there would be much studying and practicing before I would be allowed to wear the white surplice and black cassock and serve at the altar of God during mass.

It was agreed that the following Saturday after catechism class, I would stay an additional hour to start training and studying the Latin that was necessary for me to know. This was to take most of the spring and, even after being accepted as an altar boy, I had to keep on studying and training. I did become an altar boy, and the church played a big part in my life, which from time to time you will see.

We returned to find my father had arrived home while we were at church and had cooked a good breakfast for all of us. Easter this year was a very nice day. My dad then returned to Grand Rapids.

I had a week's vacation from school during which I had plenty of work around the farm to keep me busy. I carefully raked the leaves off the flower bed in the front yard so that I wouldn't break any of the tulip sprouts, dug around the spirea bushes, the two large maple trees, the backyard catalpa tree and then went on to raking the front, back and two side lawns. Next I fixed the hand lawnmower so it would be ready when the grass needed cutting, and did many other things around those ten acres of land.

One day I walked up the road about a quarter of a mile to Mr. Bracken's house. He was an old bachelor who had an old frame house on one acre of land on which he grew nothing but gladiolas.

"Hi, Mr. Bracken, I'm here to see if you need any help this spring with your flowers."

"Well, hi there, Bobby Holt. Yes, I could use some help but I wouldn't be able to pay you much, maybe twenty-five cents a day, or the equivalent of a day's wages in gladiola bulbs in the fall after we pick the flowers. Next year you could raise and sell your own flowers."

I agreed to this. His "glads" were ready to be planted. For the balance of the week I helped rake the ground, mark rows for planting, and then started to plant his gladiola bulbs. At the end of the week, I had made seventy-five cents, which I thought wasn't too bad because he would still need me off and on to help weed the flower beds and do other things.

The short vacation was over and back to school I went. Spring was really here now and my friends and I enjoyed the early morning walk to school. I never gave it a thought until many years later, but I wondered how one teacher in a one-room country school taught all eight grades, plus kindergarten. Then I remembered.

Classes started promptly, and each class came forward and sat on a long bench. Questions were asked for about twenty to thirty minutes, the class was then assigned its homework for the next day and returned to the desks in the back to study. Each grade had its chance to do the same. We were taught the four basic subjects: reading, English, arithmetic and history. We attended school from 9:00 A.M. to 4:00 P.M. each day with a fifteen-minute mid-morning break, called recess, a forty-five-minute noon break called lunch time, and another fifteen-minute recess in the afternoon. Examinations of some sort were given every week. Our report card marks were based on those examinations plus what we did in those subjects in our particular class. We were graded A, B, C, D, and E, with A being the highest grade.

If I remember correctly, teachers were well respected in the community and were dedicated persons to their professions. Their salaries at that time were between twenty-five to thirty-five dollars a month. Usually they would live at someone's house in the school district, paying around ten dollars for room and board. This didn't leave them much, yet they kept teaching and doing a good job, taking an interest in each child and putting forth all the extra interest a teacher should.

The days went by and it was May. May brought with it many lazy, loafing type of days and quite often I was caught looking out the school window day-dreaming.

I went over to old man Bushwell's to see if there was something I could do for half an hour or so after school.

"Well, hi there, Bobby. Sure, you can come here after school and run down to the pasture to bring the cows to the barn and feed the chickens and geese. I'll give you a few cents each day."

"Swell, Mr. Bushwell," I said, "when do I start?"

"How about Monday after school, Bobby?"

"I'll be here, Mr. Bushwell, you can count on it."

"Okay, Bobby, see you Monday."

Mother had made arrangements with a farmer to plow a large garden and prepare it for us in return for our letting him farm the balance of our land. Plus, he was to give us a butchered pig and some beef in the fall. She had also made arrangements with the State Conservation Department to ship us a half-dozen or so boxes of pine and spruce saplings. They were small, about six to eight inches including roots, and were sent free to be used for soil conservation purposes. I had plenty of work ahead of me for the summer.

Monday night I went to Bushwell's, got the cows into the barn, and fed the chickens and geese. I didn't like the old gander there and he didn't like me. I would tease him every chance I got which made him like me even less. I finished out the week and Farmer Bushwell gave me seventy-five cents.

Nothing much was happening and the next week started out the same as usual. Then along came Thursday, and on this particular day I was a little later than normal in getting to Bushwell's. I brought the cows in from the pasture, fed the chickens, and went into the fenced-off area for the geese. I had a pail full of corn-on-the-cob, reached down and took out an ear, and again began teasing the old gander. Old man Bushwell was in the yard watching me and hollered, "Hey Bobby, don't do that, that old gander is getting mad."

The old gander must have been watching me closely because in that instant, when I looked around, he started squawking, stretched out his long neck and beak, laid his wings to his side, and took after me. I ran, dropping the pail, but couldn't get to the gate. I turned again and ran to the opposite fence, but by this time the old gander had me by the seat of my pants. As I tried to climb the fence to jump over, the gander spread his wings, flapped them, squawked some more, and beat me with his wings. He tore out the whole rear of my pants with his beak before I was able to get over the fence. Old man Bushwell just stood there laughing like all get-out. He couldn't say a word, and laughed so much he fell on the ground. I held what was left of the rear end of my pants, and half walked and half ran the mile home.

"Hi, Bob, how did it go today?"

"Fine, Mom, couldn't be better." I squirmed my way past my mother but she saw my torn pants.

"What happened, Bob?"

"Well, Mom, I ripped my pants climbing a fence. Sorry! I guess I should have been more careful." To this day I don't think she ever found out about the gander chasing me.

I finished another couple of weeks working for old man Bushwell before school was out for the year, but I stayed my distance from the gander.

"Say, Bobby, after the oats and wheat get up this summer, would you want a job cutting the thistles out of the field?"

"Sure, Mr. Bushwell, you just let me know."

"Okay, Bobby, I will. Have fun now and have a good summer."

It was June and the last week of school. I received my report card, and passed with average grades. School was over for this year. Hooray!!

At last summer was here, and I longed for my two weeks at grandmother's house and to see my friend, Big Bob, but I knew that a lot of work had to be done first around the farm. August, which is when I went to grandmother's, seemed a long way away, so I forgot it for the moment and concentrated on helping my mother finish planting the garden, and weeding, and taking care of the crops just up.

Joe Browth and I had found a small creek about one-half mile from his house and about a mile from mine. One afternoon I told Mom I was going fishing the next morning.

"Okay, Bob, but you have no fishing pole."

"I'll make one, Mom."

I used a long, thin tree branch, put string on it for line and made a hook out of a safety pin. The pole was rather nifty, I thought.

Early the next morning I stopped at Joe's house, but he

couldn't go, so I went fishing by myself. When I got to the creek, I dug some worms for bait, sat on a log on the bank, dropped my line in about two feet of water, and waited. Every once in a while I felt a nibble but couldn't catch anything. Then along about noon I felt a tug and I had one. It was a sunfish, round about three inches in length. I had enough of fishing by this time so I left the sunfish dangling on the line and headed for home.

"Hi, Mom, look what I've got? Clean it for me and we'll have it to eat."

My mother looked at the dried-up, dirty fish with a funny expression on her face, but she cleaned it, fried what was left of it, and I ate it, all in one big bite.

A couple of days later Joe came to my place.

"Hey, Bob, let's go fishing down at the creek!"

"Yeah, Joe, you should have seen what a nice fish I caught there yesterday. That creek's got fish in it all right! Wait 'til I get my pole and we'll go."

We got to the creek and Joe said, "Bob, you know, I followed this creek through the fields aways, and it runs through that property with the nice house on it over yonder. And you know what?"

"What, Joe?"

"Well, they have goldfish in their section of the creek. Think goldfish would be good to eat?"

"I don't see why not, Joe. Let's sneak over there and try fishing from their driveway bridge beyond the house."

"Okay, Bob, but let's be quiet about it," said Joe.

Well, Joe and I sat there dropping our lines in; we caught one big goldfish, it must have been six or seven inches long at least and Joe put it in his pocket for safekeeping. We soon forgot about being quiet and sat whistling and talking. I had another bite and pulled out an orange colored goldfish just about the same time the man that lived there came running down the driveway, yelling and waving his hands at us.

"Let's go Joe!" I jumped off the little bridge and landed in the creek with Joe right behind me. We ran until we reached a woods a long distance away.

Puffing and panting Joe said, "Did you see that old grouch? You would think we were stealing or something."

"Yeah, Joe, but I guess we better quit fishing for today. What about coming back to my house and then we'll go to Sand Creek to the swimming hole and do some swimming for the rest of the day?"

"Sure, Bob, let's go! We've lost our fishing poles and fish anyway."

We finished the day by swimming in the old swimming hole and lying on the bank pulling bloodsuckers off each other. Then we started for home.

"So long, Bob, see you soon."

"So long, Joe."

Soon came strawberry-picking time and my mom and I went to work picking strawberries for Glen Cartiss on the next farm to the south of ours, also for another farmer to the west of us. We didn't do badly money-wise, getting paid five cents a quart, but it was hard work. We were on our knees all day, and sometimes it seemed to me that we would never reach the end of a row. Besides eating all the berries I wanted, and throwing a few once in a while, I was pretty well-behaved that season. Mom's being there had a lot to do with that.

Glen Cartiss had told me I could go to the Grand Rapids Market with him one morning. A few mornings later, bright and early, Mr. Cartiss, his son Frank and I, with the old Model-T Ford truck loaded with strawberries and early sweet cherries, left for the market at about 4 A.M.

We arrived at the market at 5:15 A.M., and Mr. Cartiss made arrangements for his parking spot so he could sell his berries in the open marketplace. He pulled his truck into his alloted space, uncovered the berries, and waited for people to come to the market. In the meantime, Frank and I walked around, up and down the aisles, and then down to the bridge to throw stones in the Grand River.

"Say, Frank, if your dad lets us come again, let's bring our fishpoles and do a little fishing."

"Say, that's a good idea, Bob," said Frank.

We went back to the truck and had some hot coffee and a sandwich. People were now beginning to come into the market and were going from truck to truck to look at and price the berries and whatever else the farmers might have to sell.

Mr. Cartiss left us to mind the truck while he went around checking the prices of the other peddlers' wares. While he was gone, one fancy lady came by and asked Frank how much the berries were.

"They're only ten cents a quart, lady, real nice number-one berries, fresh picked. How many do you want?"

"No thanks, sonny, I saw some others for less money that were just as nice."

Frank was disappointed, but I told him she was just an old fancy crab. He agreed, and said, "Yeah, Bob, let's give her a few berries."

"Okay, Frank, give me a handful of those berries," which he did. We both took careful aim and peppered her with nice juicy, red strawberries as she walked away from the truck.

"You boys cut that out," she yelled at us. "Who's the man in charge here?"

By this time Mr. Cartiss was back at the truck. "I'm the man lady, what can I help you with?"

"Whoever those two boys are, they just gave me a strawberry bath and I think you owe me something," she said.

Well, the lady ended up with six quarts of free berries and we ended up catching it from Frank's dad.

By about two in the afternoon we had most of our load sold, except for about four crates of berries and some boxes of cherries, so Frank's dad started "hawking."

"Sale here, berries for sale, giveaway price—seven cents a quart." This started the whole, damn marketplace to hawking. We sold ours fast and then left for home.

"We had a good day boys. I'll bring you again one of these days," and he, too, laughed about the fancy lady.

Every once in a while I went to Mr. Bracken's house to cultivate with a hand cultivator, as well as weed his gladiolas by hand. Later, when they were grown, I helped pick them and tie them in bunches of six and twelve to be sold. I was surprised at how he sold them for twenty-five to thirty-five cents a dozen to women working in stores, or to anyone on the street who wanted them, for whatever he could get. He made out pretty well with selling flowers and working the other odd jobs that he had.

I went to see old man Bushwell again.

"Hi, Bobby, looking for work?"

"Yes, Mr. Bushwell."

"Okay, Bobby, see that big field of wheat over there? Take this corn cutter, go through it and cut the tops off the thistles, and I'll give you fifty cents."

Well, I worked practically all day and got my fifty cents. Then I stopped at the Titusville Store, bought a package of bulk oatmeal, had an orange crush to drink, and still had twenty-five cents left to take home.

The last part of July the Berlin Fair at Marne opened and I thought I might be able to get some free passes for rides if I helped some of the concession owners set up their stands. I went to the fairgrounds the day before the fair opened and sure enough, truck after truck had pulled into the fairgrounds loaded with equipment. I went around and asked for jobs from different people, telling them I would take tickets for rides in place of money. This really worked. By the time late afternoon rolled around and I was ready to go home, I had tickets for the merry-go-round, the sideshows, the shooting gallery, and many more; enough to last me for the three days the fair would be there. In fact, I did this each year until I was in the tenth grade of high school. I came to know some of the concession owners quite well.

I had a really good time that year at the fair and learned a lot about showing livestock and what had to be done with the entries before anyone could win any trophies or ribbons.

It was again time to go to see grandmother and my friend Big Bob, so my mother got me ready with extra pants, shirts, socks and everything else I would need for my stay. Dad was home the day we left, which was a late Sunday evening. With Harvey and

Ed, who had arrived earlier in the day to spend a little time in the country, we all got into Ed's car and started out for Grand Rapids.

We arrived at grandmother's later in the evening and grandmother, grandad, and my aunts were glad to see us. Right away grandmother sat me down and gave me cookies and milk. Grandad joined me, but instead of having cookies and milk he sat eating an apple, using a paring knife to cut the apple into easily edible pieces.

I was then sent upstairs to bed. I slept in the rear south bedroom, with my dad's brother, Uncle N.D. As I lay in bed, I could hear the freight train's whistle in the distance as it was just coming into or leaving the train crossing about a mile away. It was a nice sound to fall asleep to on a late, summer evening.

The next morning, as I was having my breakfast and working on my third bowl of bran flakes cereal with bananas, my friend Big Bob came walking in.

"Hi, Little Bob, knew you were here. Hurry up so we can go and play."

"Hi, Big Bob, I'll be right with you. Grandmother, I'm going out to play."

"All right Bob, don't forget to be back for lunch."

Out in the backyard, across my grandmother's garden, and over the fence we went to the vacant lot where we sat down on the ground and told each other everything that had happened since last we saw each other.

"Say, Little Bob, let's go down Dickenson Street and look up Neil D. and maybe shoot some naggets."

"Swell, Big Bob, but I don't have any marbles."

"I've got enough for both of us, Little Bob, so let's go."

We found Neil at his house about two blocks away and, after handshaking, slapping each other on the back, and so forth, we came back to the vacant lot and shot marbles. Needless to say, Big Bob and I lost most all of our marbles to Neil. Finally, we broke up the game and came home to grandmother's for lunch. We then proceeded to play cops and robbers, running between our houses, screaming and yelling like wild Indians. Getting tired of this, we found that sparrows had made nests in the eaves along the rear of the house.

"Say, Big Bob, let's get rid of those sparrows for my grandmother. Those birds are no good anyway. There's a bounty on them and if you keep the heads you get paid when you turn them in to the Sheriff's office."

"Okay, Little Bob, but how are we going to get them?"

"Well, Big Bob, this must be the second batch of young. Listen, you can hear them squawking in their nests."

"Yes, Little Bob, unwind that water hose over there and I'll turn on the faucet."

I turned the water on full blast and we squirted up at the birds' nests. The pressure from the water knocked down that nest along with three or four others. When they hit the ground, we stamped on a half-dozen or so baby sparrows, while all the time the big sparrows were making all kinds of a racket. Grandmother heard the commotion and came out to see what we were doing. She chased Big Bob home, sent me in the house, and went over to Big Bob's house to give his mother a lecture.

All that afternoon I stayed in and read some old, motheaten book she had on the lives and habits of birds.

At dinner that evening, with all the family present, grandmother gave me a lecture, calling me a bad boy and saying how ashamed I should be of killing those baby sparrows. It must have lasted for about twenty minutes. My grandad didn't say a word, he just sat there shifting uncomfortably in his chair. Finally, dinner was over and I went to bed, happy to do so.

The next few days Big Bob and I had a wonderful time and we stayed out of trouble with the exception of getting dirty.

On Monday morning of the second week, I went downtown with my grandad to visit my father's office. He had now moved across the street on Monroe Avenue, opposite the Pantlind Hotel, and up on the second floor. The office consisted of three rooms, three or four old broken-down desks and chairs, and spittoons at each desk.

Dad didn't chew tobacco, but my grandad sometimes did, and the old lawyer who shared dad's office, P. I. Phillips, did.

Boy, could he hit a spittoon and make it ring. I got to know him quite well and spent many hours in his part of the office listening to him and my grandad talk about the "old days." I also would read some of his old lawbooks and ask him questions. A couple of years later it was old P.I. who saved my parents' home for them. He was a clever and intelligent lawyer, but moneywise you would say he was no success.

Late in the afternoon my dad, grandad, and I returned home, and I was off to my friend's house next door to have dinner with him.

It was still early in the evening and we wanted to go to the Burton Street movie, so I begged fifteen cents from my grandad and Big Bob got about a quarter from his folks. Grandad told us to behave ourselves, we said we would, and left. We had to pay ten cents to get in, which would leave us enough for some popcorn.

On the way to the theatre we went up the alley and climbed into the old lady's pear tree and started yelling. Sure enough, out she came with broom in hand and down we jumped, running up the alley while turning and waving at her.

Inside the theatre we got our popcorn and found a seat behind some girls about our age. We struck up a conversation with them and before you knew it, we were sharing our popcorn with them.

On our way home we talked about things we would do some day, how we would always be together, and how we would grow up and be rich and own the whole city. We both knew it was getting time for me to return to the country and it left us both with a lonely feeling.

The next few days went by fast and then Friday came and my aunts again took me downtown and outfitted me with clothes. I got another pair of overalls, and those long pants made me very happy.

On Saturday I said good-bye to my friend Big Bob.

"See you at Thanksgiving and Christmas, Little Bob."

"Okay, Big Bob, take care of yourself."

THE PLANTING OF THE PINES

With my return home mother greeted me like all mothers do, and after I got settled, she told me the pine saplings had been delivered. The old farmer on the hill had been good enough to pick up the wooden boxes from the Coopersville railroad station and bring them to our home; he had also plowed a furrow running north and south, every eight feet across the hill on the west end of the farm.

There were only four wooden boxes about six feet in length and one foot wide. I went in the back room and opened one of them; there must have been a thousand saplings in each box, all nicely packed by the Conservation Department, the average sapling being about six inches in length.

I went to the rear of our farm to see what land our neighbor had plowed. I had it all planned in my mind. I would start planting a sapling every four feet, because some would no doubt die. That night I opened the other wooden boxes, poured half a pail of water into each box and then nailed the tops back on. Then I drove nails in the ends of each box to which I fastened a long rope, so that I could pull them to the hill. I could hardly wait until Monday morning to get started with the planting.

Morning came fast. I was up at 6:00 A.M., ate the awful oatmeal mother had prepared for breakfast, asked her to take care of the chores I usually did, and then started pulling the first of the boxes to the hill. It must have taken me an hour or so but I managed to get there. Then I started planting. I planted each one by hand and, after three long days of dragging boxes and digging holes, I was finished. I had plenty of trees left, so I planted some along the fence line of the farm and some near the road on the east side of the farm near our house.

For the next few days, I continuously walked up to our hill to look at my trees, and if any of my friends were visiting, they, too, walked with me. I had dreams of a beautiful forest on the hill. Little did I know at that time just how beautiful my pine forest would grow to be.

A few years later, the pines and a few Norwegian spruce trees had reached a good height; very few had died so they were pretty thick. I cut out a section about ten by twelve feet in the center of the forest. It was a nice place to go to sit or to just stretch out on the ground and meditate. It was very peaceful to become lost in thought, with the pine trees all around, and all kinds of birds flying above, chirping in the trees. It had turned into a small, beautiful forest, where I could sit or walk through the rows of trees and talk with God. Sometimes I felt that the Heavenly Father was walking right beside me and I would many times pray and ask Him to walk with me, even though I was just a human sinner, and to stay with me all of my life though I was not always as good as I should be.

Now, some forty years later, I have paid a visit to my forest and have once again walked among the trees I planted as a youngster. I found the hideaway I had cleared, and the floor thick with pine needles, at least six inches deep. I again sat among my saplings that now must be fifty to sixty feet tall. What a beautiful place it is! I hope it will always remain this way so that I may some day walk here again, hand in hand with Christ. It would be a beautiful place from which to leave this earth for the unknown beyond.

There were plenty of things to do since it was getting near the time to return to school, but first I had to work in our garden and get the carrots, beets, cabbages, and other vegetables out of the ground and put into boxes of sand so that they could be stored for the winter months. Mother had made a deal with the farmer who had taken the eight acres from us for his own use in exchange for plowing our garden. He was to give us a calf in the spring, and in return could use the rest of the land, about one acre, for more planting.

I went to see Mr. Bracken to help him cut his gladiolas and sort all of his gladiola bulbs and bulblets. Sure enough, he kept his promise to me, and gave me some one hundred and fifty assorted bulbs, plus some money.

Then it was time to return to the Lillie School. I had heard we had a new teacher for the coming year, Mr. Magoosky. I wondered what he was like and I soon found out.

My friends, the Polish boys from a mile away, showed up at my house around 7:30 A.M. smelling of that damned Polish sausage they ate every morning.

"Hi, Fred, Carl, Jack."

"Hi, Bob," they responded. "Guess we had better get a move on and find out about our new teacher."

So we all took off up the road picking up more of our friends on the way.

"Say, Bob, let's play ball when we get there and not worry about going into school today."

"Okay, Jack, did you bring your softball with you?"

"Yeah, I brung it," says Jack. Now Jack was in the eighth grade, about seventeen years old, and a pretty good sized kid.

We reached school at about 8:45, after fooling around, throwing stones and things while walking through the woods to get there.

"Go in and get your bat, Bob, and let's start the game going."

I went to the classroom and got my bat, and Don, Guy, Lou and the rest of the boys followed me out of school. We started playing ball when all of a sudden the school bell started ringing, but no one paid any attention to it.

Finally the new teacher came out, a young man about six feet tall and very slender. He looked a little like Ichabod Crane, so we thought.

"Hey, Bob, who's that?" said Jack, meaning Mr. Magoosky.

"Oh, him over there, why that's the new schoolmarm."

"Oh, yeah? Looks like a freak of some kind. Are you sure that's the schoolteacher, Bob, or just some fool standing there watching us?"

"You boys hear the bell ring?" said Mr. Magoosky.

"Yeah," said Dan and Jack, "but can't you see we're in a ball game?"

"Well, you boys get in the schoolhouse right now and no more lipping off," said the teacher.

"Who's going to make us, teacher? Not you, that's for sure. A good wind would blow you back to where you came from," said Jack. Jack edged up to Mr. Magoosky, spit on the ground, then spit in his hands and put up his fists. "Come on teacher, make me!"

We all gathered around. Mr. Magoosky was pretty smart. "What's your name?" he said to Jack.

"My name's Jack."

"Well, Jack, I have some gloves in school, and just suppose I bring them out and we have a little friendly sparring match. Then we'll see whether we all go into the classroom or not."

"Okay," said Jack.

Mr. Ichabod Magoosky returned with two sets of thin gloves, not exactly boxing gloves. He handed a pair to Jack and put on a pair himself.

"Let's go behind the woodshed, and anything goes, okay?" said Mr. Magoosky.

"Sure," said Jack, and we started for the woodshed.

We all circled around, spit on the ground, and shouted, "Get him, Jack, and show him who's boss."

Jack rushed in, flailing his arms and fists. Magoosky just side-stepped, let two fast punches go, and Jack hit the dirt. He rolled over, groaned, got up, and rushed again and again at Mr. Magoosky, but each time he hit the ground with a thud and moaned louder and louder, swearing all the while. We all backed up, making a wider and wider circle. Poor Jack had one bloody nose, one eye half-closed, a split lip, and I'm sure a good headache.

The last time down Jack hit the dirt, rolled over, and could hardly get up. When he finally did, he took off his gloves and said, "Okay fellows, let's go to school." Nothing was ever said again about it and we all got along swell with our new teacher that year and the years that followed. In fact, he played all of the games right along with us and became a friend to us as well as our teacher.

For me, I had plenty of odd jobs that fall, along with plenty of work to do at home besides studying in the evening by kerosene lamp.

The days were shorter and Thanksgiving had come and gone. That year I had to help serve the Christmas Mass at St. Mary's and it was quite beautiful. The altar had fresh cut pine trees around it. I couldn't seem to master some of the Latin so I mumbled anything. I don't think our priest ever suspected, though.

The heavy snows came and the weather was bitter cold. It was good for skating on the frozen ponds, and the swampland in the woods which were about a half-mile from the house of my friend Joe who lived a short distance from me.

It was a beautiful, bright, and sunny Saturday morning in February and I had already eaten breakfast and finished my chores. I picked up my clamp-on skates and told Mom I was going to Joe's to do some skating.

"All right, Bob, but be sure to be home for supper. Your dad's coming from the city today."

"Okay, Mom, see you later."

Joe and I went to the swamp, built a fire, and skated the whole swamp all afternoon. "Say, Bob, my folks are going to Alpine to see one of our relatives who is bedridden. Do you want to come along?"

"Sure, Joe, I'll go."

At Joe's house his dad, mom, Joe and I got into their old Model-T Ford and left for Alpine, which was a small community about fifteen miles away. I forgot all about going home.

At Alpine we stayed and stayed until it was about 1:00 A.M. when we finally started back to Coopersville. All of a sudden Joe's mom woke up to the fact that we hadn't stopped to tell my mother and dad that I was going to Alpine with them.

It was about 3:00 in the morning when we pulled into our driveway. There were cars and trucks, the sheriff's car, and horses and sleighs up and down the road, in our yard, and all around our house. Men with rubber waders over their clothes were running all over the place. We had never seen so many people in one place before, and our house was lit up like a Christmas tree. No one seemed to pay any attention to us as we left the car at the corner and walked to the house. It seemed as if everyone was yelling at once about something, and then it dawned on us that they were looking for me.

Immediately, we walked in the front door and there was my Mom. She looked as if she was about to faint, but then she grabbed the nearest stick. I thought she was going to beat me, but one of the neighbors grabbed her. She was so hysterical she didn't know what she was doing. Finally we all settled down. My dad came in from outside with the sheriff and about twenty farmers. They had all been to the swamp, breaking ice, and walking in the icy water trying to find my body because they were sure I had fallen through the ice and drowned.

Most of the farmers had come from miles around bringing their wives and some food with them. After they warmed up a bit, being wet and half-frozen, they built fires in our front and side yards which must have been visible for miles, while my dad opened all the home brew he had in the cellar. I don't remember ever seeing any of the Hollander men drink before this, but they sure did that night. Old man Bushwell stood in a corner crying and saying, "That damn little Bobby, thought for sure we had lost him." Hours later the farmers started to leave, as they had to get home to do their morning chores.

There was no church that Sunday. I went to bed and slept all day. I stayed pretty close to home that winter, but Joe and I laughed many times about what had happened, unbeknownst to my mother and the others.

Spring came and the farmer down the road again asked us for the use of our land, bringing me a newborn male calf, which I suspected was a bribe to induce my parents to say yes. I fixed a place for the calf in our old barn, and took really good care of Brownie the bull, which is what I named him. I curried him each day, made a rope halter for him, and trained him so I could ride on his back.

I had most of our vegetable garden planted, and my two hundred gladiola bulbs as well. Each night after I got home, I walked through the garden to see if they were coming up. After about ten days I noticed the green sprouts breaking through the earth. The ice had all melted in the creeks in our area, which meant there would be good fishing and swimming in the old swimming hole again that year.

Finally, school was out and soon my gladiolas would be ready for cutting. One morning a few weeks later, I gathered about six baker's dozen, that is, thirteen flowers each, and put them in a galvanized tub of water on my wagon. I proceeded up the road to old Highway 16 near Titusville, stopped to say hello to old Pete, and then continued on until I found a spot on top of the hill where I could see a long distance down the highway. When I saw a car coming, I picked up a bunch of flowers and stood along the road holding them up for the drivers to see. After about four hours I had them all sold at fifteen cents a dozen, and I felt pretty rich. On the way home I stopped at the store to shoot the breeze with old Pete and have a soft drink to quench my thirst. I did this for about two weeks and made pretty good money on my flowers.

In the meantime, Joe and I fished the creeks, caught bullheads and sunfish, and roamed the woods playing cowboys and Indians.

I had already joined the 4-H club and was planning to enter my bull-calf Brownie in the competition at the fair in Marne that year. I went to grandmother's a little sooner than usual, since I had to be home early to register the calf.

Sure enough, when I arrived at grandmother's, there was Big Bob waiting for me. After we said our hellos and brought each other up to date on our school year activities, we were off to see Fat Hank, Big Neil, Sonny the Sun-Dance Kid, and all the rest of the gang.

Those were grand and glorious days, full of all kinds of new adventures and fun. Big Bob and I grew closer and closer during those days, much to my grandmother's dismay.

Along about Tuesday evening Big Bob and I each had a quarter, and it was agreed that we could go to the movie at

Burton Heights. Big Bob's dad had been out of the state and when he returned he brought with him a large box of assorted fire-crackers which Bob told me about just before we left the house.

"Hey, Bob, see what I've got—firecrackers. Do you want a few?"

"Yeah, let me have that great, big, red blockbuster there."

"Okay, Little Bob, but remember, if we light any of these we have to get going out of the area in a big hurry before the cops come."

"Okay, Big Bob, let's start for the show and stop to aggravate the old lady on the way."

"Swell, let's do that," Big Bob said, and off we went.

When we got to the old lady's house, we sneaked up to her apple trees on the alley side and tied a string of firecrackers to a low hanging branch. Then I waited while Big Bob took a board and scraped it across her back door, yelling, "Robbers, robbers, fire, fire—come out you old witch." Out she came with an old broom in her hand, howling her head off. She started chasing Big Bob with the broom and it was at that moment I struck a match and lit the fuse on the firecrackers. She reached the apple tree just as the firecrackers went off, which must have frightened her half to death. She bellowed and hollered and fell to the ground, rolling over and over. Big Bob and I were sure the cops would be coming soon, so we breezed down the alley in nothing flat, laughing all the way to the movie house. Once inside we settled down with a bag of popcorn, and every once in a while we looked at each other and started to laugh, thinking of the old woman rolling and tossing on the ground.

I especially remember that night. After the show, about 8:30, Big Bob and I went outside, still with the three-inch blockbuster in my pants' pocket. I was sure it would sound like an army bomb going off when it was lit, and I was trying to figure where I could successfully set it off when Big Bob got the urge to go to the bathroom.

"Say, Little Bob, I've got to get to that gas station on the corner in a hurry."

"Okay, Big Bob, I'll wait for you outside."

The service-station attendant was working on somebody's old car at the front of the station, filling it with gas from the pump. Big Bob went into the washroom which had an old-fashioned tile floor, tile walls and ceilings, and a window on one side which was part-way open. I circled around the station to look through the window, since I had already had it in my mind that if I threw the firecracker in there it sure would make one hell of a big noise. As Big Bob sat on the throne, I held the blockbuster in the window getting ready to light it. He saw it and yelled, "Don't light that damned thing here, it will blow me up." I started laughing, then lit the fuse and tossed it into the room. Big Bob was trying to pull his britches up and get out, but he had locked the door and couldn't quite make it before the firecracker went off. B O O M! All hell broke loose. The gas station attendant was just finishing putting gas into a customer's car. He was so frightened he couldn't let go of the gas hose; he was pumping gas all over the car and the ground. Big Bob dove right through the bathroom window with his pants down and was all tangled up in his clothing. I was already half a block up the street heading for an alley. Behind me I heard, "Hey, hey, Little Bob, wait for me; help me, help me." I stopped and waited until Big Bob finally got his pants up and caught up to me. Down the alley we went. We hid behind a garage so we could see what would happen next.

In about ten minutes we heard all kinds of police sirens going off. Neither of us could stop laughing even though Big Bob must have been pretty uncomfortable since he had dirty shorts by this time.

"How do you feel, Big Bob?"

"What the hell do you mean, how do I feel? You know I thought the whole damn world had blown up. Wait a minute, I hear a motorcycle coming down the alley."

"Yeah, I hear it too, must be a cop. Say, Big Bob, have you got any more of those firecracker strings?"

"Yeah, Little Bob, what have you got on your mind?"

"Well, see that cop stopping up the alley, flashing his light around? We've got time to hang those firecrackers on the corner of this garage before he gets here."

He said, "You're right, Little Bob, here, hook them on that nail there," and he passed the firecrackers to me.

"Careful, it's dark."

"Okay, they're hooked up, now let's wait for the cop to come past," I said.

Sure enough, along came the cop, real slow and flashing his light back and forth. He stopped about twenty feet from us. Big Bob poked me, pointed to the next street, took out a match, cupped it in his hands, and lit the fuse. We backed up a little and waited. The cop had just thrown his leg over the motorcycle and was getting ready to move on, when the string of about fifty crackers let loose. That poor cop fell off the cycle, lay on the ground, and started swearing. We were now moving rapidly across the lawns, over fences, down another alley, and into a woodshed in which we stayed for about a half-hour or until things cooled down, and then we went home laughing all the way. When I got home I had a glass of milk before going to bed, while telling grandmother what a good show we had seen.

The next day we told all of our friends what fun we had had and Neil laughed so hard I thought he would bust a gut. Big Bob said his shorts were so dirty he didn't dare show them to his mother, he just threw them away and promised me he would not give me any more big firecrackers.

The rest of the week went by with not much excitement and to my pleasure Big Bob was going to come home with me for a few days.

In the days to follow, I showed Big Bob my calf Brownie; we combed him and washed him each morning and his skin soon became like velvet. I even let Big Bob ride him. Brownie was sure some bull calf!

"Little Bob, you ought to win some ribbons with this bull."

"I sure should. I wish you were going to be here when the Marne Fair starts, Big Bob, we'd have fun all right."

The next day we started out by going fishing, then picked up some of the boys around the area and went swimming in Sand Creek.

"How do you like the swimming hole, Big Bob?"

"It's okay, but it's got too many bloodsuckers in it for me."

"Yeah, I agree!"

"Let's get back," said Big Bob. "It's getting late and I have to leave for home tomorrow."

On our way home a farmer's dog started following us down the road. Getting tired of seeing him behind us, I wondered what we could do to chase him away. Yelling at him didn't help. As we continued walking, I saw a fence post with some binder twine hanging from it, and close by lay an old tin can. Turning to my friend, I said, "Let's have some fun with this dog?"

"Yeah, Little Bob, I'll call him over and hold him while you tie the tin can to his tail."

I took two feet of rope, tied it to the dog's tail good and tight, and looped the other end through and around the tin can. Then we let the dog go. He started to run, jump, roll over, and bellow all the way down the road while trying to get the can off his tail. No way could he get that can off, but what a funny sight he was jumping and yipping.

"Bet he won't pester us anymore, eh, Big Bob?"

"Sure won't Little Bob, he's headed for home" and so did we.

The next day Bob said good-bye and left for the city, and, as usual, I hated to see him go.

During the next couple of weeks I washed and combed Brownie each day, and the day before the fair was to open, I was at the fairgrounds helping different people to get their show booths set up and ready for business. I also went to the livestock barns and got a stall assigned to me for my bull.

Early the next morning I started down the road toward the fairground with Brownie. When we arrived I took my bull to his assigned stall, got a bale of straw and one of hay, and made him comfortable. Then I was off to roam around the grounds, using the tickets I had earned the day before for rides, eating taffy, drinking soft drinks, and having fun. The fair lasted three days, in which time I won a blue ribbon for third place with my Brownie. The fair moved on to another town and I spent the rest of the summer doing odd jobs here and there for different farmers as well as at home.

My friend Joe and I had more time to get together and roam the woods and fields, playing all sorts of games since summer was about over and all the chores were done.

Joe's house was on one side of the road and their old barn was on the other side, with a large pasture of land around the barn which my old friend, old man Bushwell, rented for his cows to graze. Each day, late in the afternoon, he would drive his Model-T pickup to the barn, milk his cows, put the milk cans in the back of the truck, and drive home.

In the barn was a haymow on the main floor. About eight feet above was another floor that went partly over the top of where Bushwell milked his cows, and directly over that part of the barn were joists spaced every two or three feet apart, leaving that section of flooring partly open. Chickens had been going into the old barn making nests and laying eggs.

On this particular warm summer afternoon, Joe and I found four nests and in each nest were a dozen or more eggs. At first we thought we would just throw them at each other for fun, but then Joe said, "Bob, I have a good idea. Let's wait till old Bushwell comes and we'll hide in here and just loop these eggs over the joists so that they'll fall on him and the cows while he's milking. What do you think?"

"Okay, Joe, that sounds good to me."

So we tested a few eggs and sure enough, they fell just right, with some hitting the joists and then slowly dripping down to the floor below. Some of the eggs must have been old because they sure smelled when they broke open.

Pretty soon old Bushwell drove up, rounded up the six or seven cows he had, and started milking. Joe and I were well hidden behind the hay and were being as quiet as church mice. We both had gathered about four dozen eggs and first Joe would let one go, then I would let one go. This went on for a while and we could hear old Bushwell swearing a blue streak.

"Hey, you little bastards, let me get my cows milked," he yelled.

We still didn't let him know we were there. Pretty soon we ran out of eggs and thought it was about time to leave, so we crossed the road and laid down in a ditch next to the cornfield to watch.

"He's about through, Joe, but I have an idea. Get your dad's shovel up by the house and bring it back."

"Okay, Bob," he said as he headed for home.

When he got back I said, "Follow me, Joe, and stay close. See all those fresh cow flops next to the barn?"

"Yeah Bob, I get the idea," he said laughingly.

"Okay, Joe, you watch for Bushwell while I get one on the shovel. Then open the driver's door on the Model-T, but be quiet."

I scooped up a cow flop as big as a pancake, while Joe opened the truck door, and then I eased the flop to where old Bushwell would have to sit. We closed the door and returned to the ditch to wait and watch. We had timed it just right, the cows had been turned out to pasture and old Bushwell was coming with two full milk cans which he promptly tossed in the back of his truck. He was looking around as if he was waiting for something to happen, opened the truck door, jumped in, and was about to start the motor when he began to wiggle and squirm around in his seat. Putting his hand under his rump for a minute, he pulled it up and looked at it. When he realized in what he was sitting, he jumped out of his truck, swore bloody murder, and grabbed a pitchfork from the back of the truck. We didn't know what he was going to do, but we jumped up from the ditch, yelled, and took off through the cornfield heading for the woods. Old Bushwell was right behind us, swearing at us every step of the way, saying he was going to shove that pitchfork right up our behinds if he caught us. Joe and I reached the woods way ahead of him and hid out until he must have gotten tired, because a little later we heard the pickup truck's motor starting.

Joe and I started for home laughing all the way about the tricks we had played on the old man.

"Guess I better get home, Joe. See you next week when school starts and don't tell anyone about what we did today because I'll need some extra work this fall and old Bushwell usually gives me some odd jobs around his farm."

"Okay, Bob, see you Monday." With that Joe went into his house and I continued on home.

8

BROWNIE GOES TO SCHOOL

School had started and I was now in the seventh grade at the Lillie School.

I waited a couple of weeks before going to see old man Bushwell about a job because I had the feeling he might run me off the place after what Joe and I had done to him earlier that week.

One bright, sunny morning I decided that I would take Brownie my bull to school. I put his rope halter on him, took another rope with me to use to tie him up while I was in school, and since riding was better than walking, I climbed on his back, and started out. When I got to the school yard all the kids gathered around and asked me if they could ride my bull. Of course the teacher, Mr. McGoosky, didn't approve of my bringing Brownie to school, but he didn't want to send me home so told me to tie Brownie to the fence and come into the classroom while he ushered the others into the schoolhouse. I did as he said, tying Brownie to a fence post bordering old Bushwell's field next to the school.

Everything was fine until the noon hour came. After my friends and I ate our lunch we started playing ball, which must have upset the bull, because all of a sudden he snorted and started pawing the ground. Then, with a loud snort and a jerk of the rope, he loosened the fence post from the ground and all of a sudden the post and a part of the fence gave way, falling with a loud thud. Brownie started running around the school yard, scaring all the kids and Mr. McGoosky too, and finally ended up in the woodshed separating the girls and the boys outside privies. After getting him calmed down I again tied him,

64

but this time to a board on the shed. If he would have gotten excited again he probably would have pulled the whole woodshed down around his ears. After school I got him away from the woodshed and rode him home. By this time I had been told by Mr. McGoosky not to bring him back again. This ended my good idea of riding Brownie to school.

I had to go to see old man Bushwell now to make arrangements for paying for the damage done by Brownie to his fence. This, plus the fun Joe and I had earlier, cost me two days of working around old Bushwell's farm without being paid.

Later in the fall we traded Brownie to a farmer in the area in return for our winter meat. I hated to get rid of him but he had become too big and it wasn't safe to have him around the farm any more.

9

THE BOY SCOUTS

Things were getting a little dull for me and since I had heard there was a Boy Scout troop in Coopersville, I thought I would ask around about what I had to do in order to join.

One Saturday morning in late October I met our mailman, who was also the local deputy sheriff, and asked him what, if anything, he knew about the Scouts.

"Oh sure, Bobby, that would be great for you. My son Morrie belongs. Just show up in town Monday night for their meeting and I'll tell Morrie you're coming."

"Fine, Mr. Long, I'll be on the corner of Main Street near the Lillie grocery store at about 7:00 P.M."

Monday night I stood on the corner as preplanned and along came a well-built young boy about my age with another boy who had shocking red hair.

"Hi," said Morrie, "are you Bob Holt?"

"Yes, are you Morrie?"

"Yes, glad to know you. Come on, the meeting is across the street and on the second floor of that building," he said, as he pointed to a building up the street. I could see others going in. "Say, Bob, I want you to meet Howie."

"Hi, Howie," I said.

"Hi, Bob, glad to know you. How did you get here?" I told him I had walked to town. "Well, let's go," he said, and we started across the street.

The meeting lasted a good hour and a half in which I was accepted, initiated, and became a full-fledged Boy Scout. Our meetings were once a week on Monday nights. I would walk

66

the two miles to Coopersville and two miles home until I finally bought a used bicycle for five dollars.

I kept up with the meetings for two years, going to a scout camp for a week during each summer. That really was nice for me since I made a lot of new friends with whom I renewed acquaintances when I eventually entered Coopersville High School. Howie was one of them, and he later became one of my closest friends during our school days.

The Boy Scouts had taught me how to live and how to survive in the woods, how to build fires without matches, how to canoe and swim, and many more useful things. It was a most enjoyable part of growing up.

Thanksgiving and Christmas had passed that year without any problems. Prohibition had now been repealed, but mom and dad still had their parties with their friends from the city, except for Big Dutch who, dad said, had been "sent up the river."

10

THE SHIVAREE

When my friend Bushwell's wife died, he started dating an old sweetheart of years gone by. After a few months they decided to get married.

Ours was an old-fashioned community and when there was a wedding in the country in those days, everyone participated in a grand celebration called a shivaree. Even today it is still held in some parts of the country.

About four in the afternoon, after the wedding, thirty men and boys, myself included, showed up in the backyard of old Bushwell's farm. Each of us brought either an old galvanized washtub or bucket, and clubs to beat them, and anything else we could drag along that would make noise. Some of the men brought shotguns to fire in honor of the wedding.

The first thing we did was to help Bushwell with all of his chores. Then we pushed and dragged him to his house, and once inside we tried to keep him from his bride. Some of us held Bushwell while the others tried to catch the bride with thoughts of locking her in the barn or chicken coop. She was faster than we thought she was. We weren't able to get her outside so we left her in the house with old Bushwell and sealed all the doors shut so neither could get out. It was such a bitter cold winter day that we outside built a number of fires in the yard just to keep warm.

Then it started—the beating of washtubs and wash basins with sticks, shotguns going off left and right, horns blowing, yelling and dancing, and anything else we could think of that might disturb the happy couple. This went on for about an hour. Finally, old Bushwell opened a window and started yelling.

Everything became quiet so that we could hear what he had to say.

"If you guys will quit now, I'll give you fifteen dollars," he yelled.

"No good," said Big Hank, "it's not enough. Okay, fellows, on with the show."

For the next two hours the racket went on and on. More offers were made by Bushwell and turned down by us. Meanwhile more and more people were arriving until there must have been sixty or seventy of us in all.

At two in the morning an upstairs window opened and old Bushwell stuck out a white sheet which he started waving at us. We all stopped our hell-raising once more to hear what Bushwell's new offer would be.

"Hey, Hank, I have three cases of beer, five large bottles of whiskey, some corn bread my new wife made, along with chocolate cookies, candy bars, and hot coffee, plus I'll still give you the fifteen dollars."

Hank yelled back, "How about making it twenty-five dollars?"

"Okay," yelled old Bushwell as he closed the window.

We unnailed the doors and most of us that could went inside to prance around and see the new wife. What a fine heifer she was, a little old and plump, I thought, but just right for my friend old Bushwell.

"Say, Bobby," said old Bushwell, catching me taking a drink of whiskey, "that's not for you. Take some candy and cookies instead."

"Leave the kid alone," said Big Hank, "he's been out in the cold and some whiskey won't hurt him a bit. Here, take a good slug, Bob, you're big enough now to tip the bottle."

Well, for the next hour we ate, drank, and sang, some of us getting quite drunk, and all of us wishing old Bushwell and his new wife the very best and many happy years together. By four in the morning the last of us were leaving for home, much to the relief of Mr. and Mrs. Bushwell, I'm sure. As hectic as the shivaree was, I still think old Bushwell and his bride had as much fun as we did.

11

THE BRIDGE AND THE RIVER

For many months during the winter my mother talked about getting baby chicks to raise and perhaps sell their eggs to the stores in both Coopersville and Marne, but the question was—how to get the chicks without money? She wanted to buy three hundred chicks since we had a brooder that would house at least that number, and was equipped with a stove to keep the chicks warm and get them through the winter.

My mother, being a proud woman, wouldn't seek to borrow the money from my granddad, but instead, one early Monday morning, dressed herself and me, left my sister and brother with Mrs. Picket across the road, and we walked to Titusville and Highway 16 to see if we could get a ride from a passing motorist. Each time a car came along I would put my thumb out until we finally secured a ride which took us into downtown Grand Rapids. When we got there, we went to my dad's office where I sat around talking to grandad, and of course, my friend old P. I., the lawyer.

After a while mom and I left the office and started going from bank to bank, trying to borrow enough money to buy those chicks she wanted so badly. By mid-afternoon we had visited every bank in town and then started back to my dad's office. Mother was all in and very down in the dumps as she had not been able to get a loan anywhere. With the expression on her face, I thought she would start crying at any moment. We sat there for a few minutes while she told my dad what had happened, and then we left for home.

We started walking to Leonard Street, which was Highway 16, and from there it was about three miles to the outskirts of town where we would again try to get a ride to take us back to the farm. As we approached the long bridge that crossed over the Grand River, I noticed my mother's face. It was as if I could read her thoughts. I knew that she was contemplating suicide. I took her hand as she stopped and leaned against the wall of the bridge looking at the cold water below. We soon moved on to about the center of the bridge where she stopped again and again and stood looking down at the river. I knew my mom must have been feeling very low in spirit right then. The years of the Depression and struggle must have gotten to her. As I stood there looking up at her, I had an awful fear inside of me that she was going to try to jump off the bridge and into the river. Again I reached out and took her hand.

"Mom, don't do what you're thinking, please, we all love you very much and need you."

Mother looked down at me for what seemed like a very long time, then tears came to her eyes and she stooped over and put her arms about me hugging me as tight as she could. She mumbled, "My son, I was ready to give up but I know it would have been very foolish of me. We will survive somehow. We'll get there someday, Bob, it's not the end of the world."

She straightened up and wiped her eyes, then took my hand as we continued on across the bridge. I was still frightened as we walked the rest of the distance across the bridge and down the street to the highway where we thumbed another ride home. I was sure relieved to get back to the farm.

I never wanted to walk across the river again with my mother since that time, not under any circumstances. What happened that day really stuck in my mind. To this day I don't think mother realizes what happiness she has added to all of our lives over the years. Mother nor I have ever mentioned that incident to this day.

When Saturday came, my father, Harvey, and my grandad arrived for the weekend. Grandad gave my mother the needed money with which to buy the baby chicks and extra money to buy their feed and whatever else they might need. The following week mom finally got to order her chicks from the hatchery.

Three weeks later a truck drove into the yard with boxes and boxes of newborn chicks. Then the work began, feeding, watering them so that they would remain healthy. The first few weeks of a baby chick's life finds them in quite a delicate condition. If they don't have clean water and the right amount of food and heat in the brooder house, they could get diarrhea and die—one after another. After much time and care we finally had them past the danger point and on the way to being pullets, which are young hens either used to lay eggs or for human consumption. Mother decided to look around for a buyer for some of the hens. Mr. Charman, the man who owned the grocery store in Coopersville, offered a good price for the chickens so she sold them, making a very handsome profit. She did, however, keep fifty hens for us so that we would have fresh eggs for ourselves.

12

THE LAWYER

For some time now the former owner of our small farm, who held a small note on the property, had been after my dad for payment of that note. Dad had plenty of financial difficulties, as did everyone else, and though he was always able to take care of them, this man was pressing my father pretty hard, threatening to foreclose and take back his property.

We had been served legal papers by my friend Farmer, the lawyer who lived on the farm on the hill north of us.

On this particular Saturday night, my dad and my friend old P. I. Phillips, the bachelor lawyer who had his office and living quarters next to my dad's office, arrived. P. I. looked a sight; his old worn-out suit was all wrinkled, and he was wearing an old coffee-stained tie with a shirt that looked even older than his suit. My mother made him take his suit and shirt off so she could wash and press them. She threw away his tie and gave him one of my dad's to spruce him up a little.

I remember my father walking into the kitchen looking as white as a ghost, worried half to death about losing our home. That was the second time this had happened and mother told me in later years that she was afraid dad was going to have a stroke due to his worrying about us and the farm.

Monday morning came and off my dad and old P. I. went. I too, left, but for school, and even though I was there in body, my mind was on my father and what could happen to all of us if we lost the farm. Even though I was a young boy, I worried all that day.

When I got home that afternoon my mom seemed more relaxed and in a very good mood. After awhile we went outside to watch the sunset and sit on the cold cement porch and chat.

73

She told me that old P. I. had settled everything and that he had saved our home for us. There would be no more to worry about in that area. According to her, he saved our home through a long court battle and won the case because of several words that had been initially placed in the land contract which prevented the owner from foreclosing on the property. Anyway, the landlord was beaten and didn't get the farm. It seemed that he had already been paid in full several months before, but thought he was entitled to more. My mother told me she thought Old Slaughter, the one I called Farmer, didn't put up too much of a fight for his client. She suspected he wasn't in sympathy with his client and I always felt that somehow he lost so that my folks would not have to move. Anyway it was over, and we paid old P. I. by bringing him chickens, vegetables and fresh meat whenever we had some to spare.

Dad always said old P. I. was a great lawyer, educated and intelligent, but the Depression was so bad that he couldn't make any money at his chosen profession. He was forced to live in his office because he couldn't afford to rent a home or pay for lodgings. He died without a dime in his pockets, but his life was certainly not a waste. Many people, poor and rich alike, were at his funeral, with nothing but good things to say about him. People were talking afterwards and from what I gathered, they thought old P. I. could have been a wealthy man in his day but was too good-hearted to people. He knew his clients were in the same financial straits that he was and he would more often than not be paid in material goods instead of cash, as we had paid him. Thus ended the life of a good friend, a good lawyer, and a true humanitarian.

13

THE BUM

School was out and besides my work at home I had kept quite busy working a day or two here and there for the different farmers in the area so it seemed as if the summer went by quite fast that year. Finally, the latter part of summer arrived and I was off to grandmother's for my annual visit. Of course this meant I would see my good friend Big Bob. I arrived late Monday night and received the usual hugging and kissing from both of my grandparents, then cookies and milk, and then I was put to bed.

Early the next morning Big Bob was waiting for me in the front yard as he had done so many times in the past.

"Hi, Little Bob," he greeted me.

"Hi, Big Bob, what's new?" After he had told me what he had done with himself all summer, I then told him what I had been doing. "Big Bob, I can only stay through Friday this time because now I'm a Boy Scout and am spending a week at the Boy Scout camp this year."

"Gee, Little Bob, I'm sorry to hear that! Let's go see the gang."

"Okay," says I as we started off to find Neil, Hank, and the Sun-Dance Kid. We found our pals just down the road, getting ready to start a ball game. After the usual hand shaking and back slapping, we started the game which lasted all that day.

On the way home Big Bob said, "Say, Little Bob, I got me a girl." This rather took me by surprise.

"Yeah, what's her name?"

"Marjorie," said Big Bob. "We'll go to see her after supper."

"Okay, Big Bob, see you later."

After supper we met outside and started down the alley, across the vacant lot into Dickinson Street, and up to Marjorie's house, where we sat on the porch waiting until she came outside. After the introductions were over we all sat and talked. I hit it off with her right away. She was a small, blonde girl, very sweet, and seemed to be full of fun. I nodded my friend my approval. Marjorie remained his girlfriend for the next few years until they married in 1940, with me as best man at the wedding.

The following morning Big Bob came over bright and early and we played in grandmother's backyard for a while, running between the houses, yelling and screaming, and acting like two little Indians. We soon got tired of that and wondered what else we could do that would be exciting.

"Say, Little Bob, let's go to the railroad yard and see if we can pester the railroad cops." I thought this was a swell idea, so we went down the street toward the old circus grounds which preceded the railroad yards.

Walking along the tracks, Big Bob stopped, held his finger up to his mouth in a hushing fashion, and pointed to a small clump of trees and high brush up ahead.

"See there, Little Bob, that looks like smoke. Let's check it out."

"Okay, Big Bob, let's crawl through the grass, somebody might be there."

We wormed and eased our way up to the thicket, quietly pushing some of the high weeds to the side so we could peer through. Sure enough, there was a man dressed in a tattered, blue pin-striped suit, a blue and white patterned vest, equally as tattered, a dirty white shirt with a small, red bow tie, and a pair of worn brown shoes with no socks. There he sat on a box near a little bonfire, holding a can of something on the end of a stick and dangling it over the fire.

Bob and I looked at each other and he said to me, "Be quiet, he could be a bank robber or a murderer or something, and if he catches us maybe we'll never get home again."

"Yeah, Big Bob, let's watch him for a while. Do you suppose there's a reward for him?"

Just then Big Bob sneezed and jumped, snagging his foot in a hole and falling through the brush face down in the circled area right at the man's feet. The man was quick to reach out and grab Big Bob by the arm, holding him tightly.

I then stepped into the circle saying, "Let my friend go or I'll hit you with this stick," which I grabbed from the underbrush.

"Oh, there's two of you, eh! Don't be afraid of me, I'm just a harmless old bum. What are you two boys doing here anyway?"

Somehow he didn't seem as threatening as he did before, so we sat down and started talking to him, telling him we were just roaming around and thought we would run in and out of boxcars for a while.

"You boys shouldn't do that. The railroad cops will get you."

"Oh no, they won't," I said, and then I asked him his name.

"Just call me the bum," he said. "I never give my name to anyone. Here, try some of these beans." He passed us his stick with the dangling can.

We ate a few scoops of beans and then started asking him questions about what it's like to be a bum. We learned that he rode in open boxcars or sometimes under the train—fitting himself snugly up and around the crossbars. He went where he pleased and when he pleased, ate whatever he could get, slept any place he could, and didn't have a worry in the world. According to him he was as free as a bird with the exception of having to watch for the railroad cops. If they caught him they would give him a bad time and see to it that he was locked up for vagrancy.

Just about this time we heard men coming down the track.

"Hey, boys," said the bum, "they've spotted my fire so let's get out of here."

The bum grabbed his knapsack and we all ran toward a little wooded area near the circus grounds. The cops had now seen us and were in hot pursuit, but then the bum spotted a freight train pulling out of the yard and off we went trying to catch up with it. The bum reached it first, jumped into an open boxcar, and then started yelling to us to hurry up. We finally made it and he reached down and gave us both a hand and pulled us up beside him. By the time the cops got to where we were, the train was moving too fast for them to do anything. We all three sat on the edge of the boxcar, thumbed our noses with one hand, and waved good-bye to the cops with the other. Now our problem was where were we going and how were we going to get back.

"How are we going to get off this damn train, Little Bob?"

"I don't know. Maybe we'll end up in New Orleans and become bums ourselves, wouldn't that be keen?"

Big Bob agreed with me, so we just sat there enjoying the ride, talking and laughing. I think the bum enjoyed having us around for a little while. Soon he told us that about three miles from where we were the train came to a small town called Granville, and then it slowed down to almost a stop.

"When we get there you boys get ready, and when I tell you to, jump and roll down the embankment. You'll be able to walk home in about two hours' time. You don't really want to be bums. You would miss your homes and families too much."

I think he was trying to tell us a little of how he felt at times. He sure knew what he was talking about. Pretty soon the train began to slow down and the engineer started blowing the train whistle; we were coming into Granville.

"Now get ready," said the bum, and, with a "good-bye my little friends," he gave us both a hard push, and the next thing we knew we were lying at the bottom of a ditch, scratched and bruised, but otherwise all right. Now we were sure we didn't want to become bums.

It took us a long time but we finally got back to our homes.

"Little Bob, you had better tell your grandmother you got those bruises falling in a brush pile. If she or my mother knew where we had been and what we had done, we would both get skinned alive." I knew he was right so we both agreed to stick to that story.

"I'm going to bed early tonight, see you in the morning, Big Bob." With that I went into the house, washed myself, and ate supper, all the while managing to stay out of my grandmother's way. Then I retired pretty early. Now that I think of it, she must have thought I was sick.

The week passed without much else happening. At the week's end I said good-bye to Big Bob and his girlfriend Marjorie, telling them I would see them at Thanksgiving or Christmas.

"Okay, Little Bob, so long for now," they said, and I went back to the country and home.

14

THE LAST YEAR AT
A ONE-ROOM COUNTRY SCHOOL

That September was my last year at the Lillie School. I didn't
realize then that it was the best time of life, as most people
don't realize, but many years later, I awakened to the fact that
those were my happiest days.

In early October in that part of the country, cooler weather
was on its way. Walking to school down a country gravel road
was an exhilarating experience with the crisp wind gently
brushing my face, the sound of rustling trees all around, and
frosted-over rain puddles along the edge of the road, reflecting the
sun like a thousand diamonds. The most fun was stepping on
these patches of ice and feeling them crunch beneath my feet.
The sun rose out of the east and the air had a cool, crisp, clean
smell to it. The birds gathered in the open fields, getting ready
to go south for the winter, and the trees were just beautiful, with
all the magnificent colors that artists have tried to capture for so
many years.

We had a new priest come to the parish about three months
before, a big, strapping Irishman, called Father Tweeney. Father
Tweeney had been at our home several times since he arrived in
town, and my dad liked him so much that when he was home
on weekends he started going to church again. This made my
mother very happy.

That priest taught me many things about our religion. One
Sunday after mass he called me into the sacristy to tell me that
when I mumbled he knew it was because I didn't know my Latin
and I had better learn it. I had also made a mistake on Sunday
on the altar by moving the Gospel Book when it wasn't the proper

time. He really lectured me on that, and I will always remember it.

"Bobby, if you make a mistake don't do it halfway. Make the mistake all the way and carry it through. Never do anything halfway. Do you understand?"

"Yes, Father Tweeney," I said.

"All right, Bobby, see you next Sunday." Next Sunday was the church dinner.

It was in October that St. Mary's Church had what we called a potluck dinner to help raise money for the church. All the women of the parish brought different foods and cooked them in the church basement. Tickets for this affair were fifty cents per person, though altar boys got in free.

The Saturday before the church dinner, my friend Big Bob came out to the farm from the city with my dad. Mother had worked at the church all that day preparing her contribution, so Big Bob and I spent the day roaming through the woods, climbing trees, and talking about what we would eat the next day.

"Say, Big Bob, they will have soft drinks and bingo under the big tent, and I hear they're going to sell beer too. Have you got any money with you?"

"Sure, Little Bob, about a dollar and a half."

"Oh, that should be plenty," I said.

Sunday morning we all went to church, mother, dad, my sister, brother, Bob, and myself. After mass Big Bob and I went out and looked around the grounds. We met Joe, Harry, and some of the other fellows, and proceeded to look for the tent with the soft drinks. We stood around for a while, drinking our soft drinks and watching the people passing by, until Big Bob spotted some dry ice and thought it would be a good idea to bet the rest of us that he could hold a piece of dry ice on his arm longer than we could. We each bet five cents. I took a piece of ice and held it on my arm, but it began to sting so badly that I threw it away. Big Bob did hold his the longest, but it burned his arm and left a scar about two inches long, which he carried all of his life.

Then we went in to the dinner, and ate until we were ready to burst. When we got home, Big Bob and my dad left immediately for the city. I told Bob to keep that bandage on his arm so that the burn would heal.

"I'll be okay, Little Bob. See you in a few weeks," and they drove out of the yard.

Thanksgiving and Christmas came and went. During that time I saw my friend and his girlfriend, Marjorie, and all the rest of the gang. Big Bob was sure proud of his scar. He showed it to almost everyone.

The new year was going fast and I would soon be graduating from grade school. This year I had been promised a job by one of the farmers named Alton who lived about fifteen miles from my house. I would live there for the season, getting my room and board, plus twenty dollars a month. I was anxious for the summer to come, since I enjoyed working with the soil, and that twenty dollars looked mighty good to me.

It was now late spring and graduation time. We were holding our graduation ceremonies at the Dutch Reformed Church in Coopersville, a nice little church close to the main section of the town. It was a big day for me, and now that school was over, I knew I would never forget that one-room country schoolhouse.

15

HIRED FARMHAND

I had now arrived at Alton's two-hundred-acre farm and was given a room upstairs in the farmhouse for my belongings. The chores, as explained to me, consisted of milking some fourteen cows each morning and evening and tending a few horses, one large bull, about three hundred chickens, and several pigs. After rising at six the next morning and milking the cows all by hand, we took care of feeding of the rest of the animals, as well as cleaning their pens and coops. When this was done, we went in to a breakfast of ham, fresh eggs, pancakes, fried potatoes, and good strong coffee. Mrs. Alton sure knew how to cook.

Afterwards, we went to the fields with a team of horses and began disking and dragging the different fields. I got used to walking behind the horses with the straps from the cultivator wrapped around my waist to keep the horses going in one direction, at the same time holding the handles of either the cultivator or the drag to guide it also.

The apple and peach orchards had to be dragged about once a week for a six-week period, along with a once a week spraying. The spraying was a real hassle. We put a large spray barrel full of insecticide on a horse-drawn wagon. We drove up and down the rows of trees, stopping at each one to spray it from a pipe attached to the barrel. All of this was done before supper, which was about 6:30 P.M., along with unharnessing the horses, watering, and feeding them. After supper we did the evening milking and finished up the rest of our chores. If we were lucky we were finished by 8:00 P.M. This went on all summer long.

Mr. Alton's father lived about a mile down the road from

him with six other sons, the youngest by the name of Pat. Pat was a year or two older than myself and he would come to the Altons' house every evening around 8:30, and we would sit and talk, or play, or do something.

One evening, we took an old water trough and hooked it up to the top of the garage, attached a hose to the small opening on the bottom of the trough, and filled it with water. We didn't have an indoor shower but thought we would try this to see if it worked. It did. In the day the sun heated the water, and at night we both stripped and took a shower. Boy, that felt good!

One day all six of the Alton boys were visiting their married brother, and young Pat brought along a pair of boxing gloves. Pat was about six feet tall and weighed somewhere around 170 pounds. He asked me if I would like to box with him.

"Sure Pat, let's go upstairs in the barn."

He agreed, and we proceeded to the barn with all of the brothers right behind us. After putting on our gloves, we sparred with each other for a while with me ducking Pat's punches as best as I could, because I knew if he hit me, I would probably fly right through the side of the barn. I kept dodging and ducking until all of a sudden I said, "Hey, Pat, better check your shoelace, it's untied."

Pat stopped and looked down at his feet and at that very instant I let him have a left—just on the side of the head and crossed with a hard right to the face, another left to the head, and two more to his stomach. He sat down, kerplunk, on his fanny and his nose started to bleed; but he soon got up and took a playful swing at me.

Then he said, "Say, Bob, you've gotten me all tired out, what do you say we quit for today?"

"Sure Pat, I've had it too. In fact, if you would have hit me like that, I would have been hearing birds singing."

We boxed many more times after that, and I somehow always managed to keep away from his punches. If he ever would have hit me, I know it would have been curtains for me. Pat was as strong as a bull.

There were all German farmers in that section of the country, and they were known for their capacity to drink. Later in the summer, from working with them, I, too, learned how to hold my liquor and not get drunk. The Altons brought out to the fields a milk can filled with a mixture of half cider and half wine and loaded with ice, so that whenever anyone was thirsty, he took a scooper full. As powerful as this drink was, I never saw any of the boys intoxicated, except for Big Arnie once in a while. When Big Arnie, about six feet two inches and weighing two hundred and seventy-five pounds, had too much to drink, the rest of the boys would see him safely home.

Big Arnie was something else. I once saw him lift up a corner of a filled hay wagon about three feet in the air, to help a team of horses get across a mud hole, which was on an incline leading into the barn. That's how strong a man he was.

One day toward the end of summer, we were bringing hay from another farm three miles away to the Alton's farm and somebody was lagging behind.

Big Arnie said to me, "Bob, take my old car and drive to the farm, give those guys hell, and tell them to hurry up. We want to finish sometime today."

"Okay, Arnie, I'll be back later."

This was great for me. I had never driven a car before, but I knew all you had to do was to get in, turn the key to start the motor, step on a couple of floor pedals, shift gears, steer the wheel, and you were driving. Well, I got to the other farm, delivered the message, and started back. On the way I wanted to see what the old car would do so I opened up to about forty miles an hour. When I got to the turn just before the Alton's farm, I hit loose gravel and the car skidded, hitting a wire fence guard-line at the edge of the road. It continued on, tearing out four posts, rolled down a six-foot embankment, and stopped in an upright position. After I caught my breath, I started it up again and drove it to the farm yard with a banged-up fender and door.

There stood Arnie with the other boys, all of them as white as a sheet. They had heard the noise and knew I must have had an accident. I was afraid to get out of the car, since I thought Big Arnie was going to give me the licking of my life. Instead, he walked over to the car, opened the trunk, and pulled out six sticks of dynamite and a paper bag full of loose detonating caps. I almost fainted.

"That's the end of your driving my car, Bob, you could have blown yourself up. We'll forget about the damages, I'm just glad you're not hurt."

I sure felt bad about banging up Arnie's car, but I learned my lesson. No more hot-rodding for me.

The summer now was at an end and it was time for me to go home. I left with close to fifty dollars, enough to buy my books and clothes for school that fall and still have about fifty cents a week to spend.

I really missed not going to grandmother's house that year and not seeing Big Bob, but all in all I had a very good summer.

16

SMOKING

My friend Joe and I used to walk to St. Mary's Church on Saturdays. He would either walk to my house and we would leave from there, or I would meet him at Titusville and we would walk the three miles.

One Saturday, while walking along the highway, we decided to try smoking. We had already tried corn silk wrapped in newspaper and thought it wasn't too bad.

"Hey, Bob, there's a cigarette butt, do you want to try smoking it?"

"Sure, Joe, let's collect some."

We started collecting thrown-away cigarette butts until we both had a handful, then we lit them up one after the other, and puffed away.

"It's not too bad, Joe. Here, I have a long one. Whoever smoked this cigarette didn't smoke much of it before tossing it away."

We got to the church a little early with plenty of cigarette butts in our pockets. We knew we couldn't smoke them in church, so we went to the outside privies and smoked up a storm. By the time our class started, we were both rather pale. We sat through the class with Father Tweeney looking at us kind of funny every now and then.

"Is something the matter with you boys?"

"Nope," I said, "but I have a kind of headache."

Father Tweeney apparently believed me because he didn't say any more about it. From that time both Joe and I smoked off and on that way.

About a week or so after that church incident I was playing by the barn with my brother Bim. I had already gotten some dry corn silk from the cornfield and had rolled a long, good sized cigarette out of it. I took Bim behind the barn, lit the cigarette and stuck it in his mouth.

"Okay, you little snitch, you're always going to tell mom that I smoke, now you smoke this or I'll beat you up."

I made him smoke it all and he got so sick I thought he was going to die. When mother found out what I had done, she went straight outside, pulled a small branch off the closest tree and whipped me until my legs and backside were black and blue. That ended my smoking career around the house, but I continued away from the house. Mother never said any more about it, but I suspect she could smell smoke on me once in a while. Anyway, I didn't try to make my little brother smoke any more.

It was now getting late in the fall and the thrashing and harvesting of wheat for the farmers in our area was about over. I had heard my friend old man Bushwell still had his harvesting to do and thought I might ask him for a job.

17

THE STRAW STACK

Friday night after school I walked the extra mile from Coopersville High to my friend Bushwell's house and asked him for a job. I had heard the farmers were coming Saturday to finish up his wheat harvest.

"Well, Bobby, I think I have all the help I need."

"Okay, Mr. Bushwell, I just thought I would ask," and I started to walk away.

"Say, Bobby, I do need someone to build a straw stack for me, but I can't pay much. Do you suppose you could do it?"

"Well, Mr. Bushwell, that's quite a job. I've seen it done but I don't know if I could do it."

"I'll give you seventy-five cents," he said. I thought it was at least a five-dollar job, but then I pondered it for a couple of minutes and decided to do it.

"All right Mr. Bushwell, I'll do it, but that's mighty cheap." He laughed and said he would see me around seven in the morning.

A straw stack is built from the base in a circle about fifteen to twenty feet in diameter and ranges from fifteen to twenty-five feet in height. Teams of horses and wagons drive up to a thrashing machine and pitch wheat bundles onto a conveyor that goes through the machine. The machine separates the wheat stalks from the grain, and then blows the wheat straw from a long pipe to a straw-stack builder. The builder continuously spreads the straw in a circle, making the stack higher and higher until it is finished. Farmers use this straw to put in the animal pens during the winter months.

I showed up right on time. Ten or twelve farmers were already there with their wagons, ready to go into the fields to gather wheat. After their wagons were loaded, they would return to the thrashing machine one after another until all of the grain was thrashed. It was an all day affair.

Old man Bushwell had the place marked where he wanted the stack to be built with the thrashing machine standing next to it. I picked up my pitchfork and waited.

"Say, Bobby," said Hank, one of the farmers who came to help Bushwell, "are you going to build this stack?"

"Sure, Hank, I agreed to do it for Mr. Bushwell."

"Damn that old coot anyway, that's not a job for a boy. It takes a full-grown man to build a stack." Hank saw Bushwell and continued to cuss him out and told him that if anything happened to me he would run a pitchfork right up his rear end.

The wagons were starting to come in, one after the other. I pulled a bandana over my mouth and tied it around the back of my head, so that I wouldn't be breathing the straw dust. As the wheat stalks were flying out of the thrasher, I kept building that stack until it was three quarters as high as the barn and twenty-five feet across. What a stack that was! Finally, around 5:00 P.M., it was finished. I rolled off the top and just lay at the bottom of the stack on the ground. I was so exhausted I thought I would never get up again. Old Bushwell gave me my seventy-five cents. I said never again would I build a stack for seventy-five cents. I took off down the road, listening to some of the farmers really cussing Bushwell out.

I was sick all that night and all the next day, but I didn't tell my mom why. Still, I recovered and was seventy-five cents richer. Later, some of the farmers told me that was the best built straw stack in the territory. Was I proud!

18

HALLOWEEN IN THE COUNTRY

Halloween in the country was always a big time for kids from twelve to twenty. On this particular Halloween Joe came over about seven in the evening and we went looking for some fun.

"Say, Joe, let's go down the road and coon watermelons out of old man Picket's watermelon patch."

"Okay, Bob, that should be fun," he said.

So we went across the road, through Picket's apple orchard and into the garden, slinking around and tapping different melons with our fingers to find which cantaloupes and watermelons were ripe. We took a few melons over to the weeds next to the garden and broke them open and started eating them.

We were eating our third watermelon when old man Picket came out on the porch. We could see him in the moonlight and in his hand he was carrying his shotgun. Up we sprang, dropping the melons. We started running as fast as we could. I got to the fence first, with Joe running behind me, yelling, "Wait for me Bob." Just then Mr. Picket let loose with a shotgun full of rock salt. Joe was really screaming now, as we ran through the peach orchard some distance away. We stopped and hid behind a large tree.

"Bob, that old bastard shot me full of rock salt and does my butt burn."

"Say, Joe, I know what, let's get even with him. We'll wait awhile and then sneak back and tip over his outside privy."

"Okay, Bob, that's a good idea. Then let's walk to Coopersville and see what's going on in town."

We waited some fifteen minutes before we did anything, and

all the while Joe rubbed his behind. Then we sneaked up, got behind the privy, and pushed and pushed until the damn thing finally tipped over. Poor Joe, besides getting rock salt in his butt, he slipped one foot into the hole where the privy was. But we didn't stick around to see Mr. Picket's face. Instead, we hitailed it up the road to Coopersville, and all along the way we pushed over other farmers' outside privies. We must have turned over seven or eight of them before reaching the main street of town.

The main street looked like a disaster area. There were corn shucks, watermelons, tomatoes, and cabbages all over the street. Besides that, the merchants' windows were soaped from top to bottom. Running into some of our school chums, we joined in the fun.

"Hey, Bob," said Howie the red-headed boy, "do you and Joe want to join our gang?"

"Sure, Howie," I said.

"Okay, come on, we're going to have a tomato and egg fight with those guys over there."

We climbed up on the roofs of the buildings on one side of the street, while the other gang went up on the roofs of the buildings across the street, and then we started. We must have thrown tomatoes and eggs across the street at each other for an hour. Finally the town had had it. Joe and I left for home, but had promised to help clean the streets the next day, which we did.

On Halloween something like that would happen every year, but the boys always cleaned up the mess afterwards. We never really damaged anyone's property with the exception of toppling privies, which usually gave the people a good excuse to clean them out and put them upright again.

Joe sure stunk that night, and the next day when I saw him he said his mother wouldn't let him in the house until he got a bucket of water and washed himself from head to foot.

Boy, Halloween was fun! We couldn't wait until the next Halloween rolled around.

19

THE DANGEROUS LAKE,
THE STRANGE PRIEST,
AND THE GOLD CROSS

Thanksgiving and Christmas had come and gone, and for some reason I was going to visit my grandparents during the second week in February. That meant I would see my good friend Big Bob again.

Sometime in November, an Ottawa Indian chief and some of his tribesmen visited our high school to put on a show in the gymnasium, and asked for a volunteer to be initiated into the Ottawa tribe. My friends Howie and Merrill gave me a shove, and sure enough I went up on the stage. All the Indians danced around me, poking at me and rubbing paint on my face, and, in general, made me a real mess. They finally picked me up, held me upside down, and ran in a circle, with me in that position, while chanting and yelling. They then proclaimed me a warrior of the Ottawa tribe, to be known as Little Crow to my Indian brothers. For weeks afterwards, whenever my friends saw me, they started hooting and hollering and asking me what Little Crow was going to do now. I had fun anyway, even if my friends wouldn't let me forget "me heap big warrior."

February came and I spent three days with my grandparents and my friend Big Bob. We met, as usual, outside grandmother's house.

"Hi, Little Bob, I'm skipping school tomorrow so that you and I and Neil can take off to the woods by Green Lake."

"Okay, Big Bob, see you in the morning."

The next morning we all met in the vacant lot. "Say, Big Bob," I asked, "how's Marge?"

"She's fine, Little Bob, we'll be getting married one of these days."

"Good, I'll be your best man."

"Okay," he said, and we all headed for Green Lake.

When we arrived, we promptly built a fire at the edge of the lake. The lake was frozen over so that we could walk anywhere we wanted to. After sitting around the fire for some time, Big Bob bet he could cut a hole through the ice and dive to the bottom, coming right back up through that hole.

"Well you better not, Big Bob, or you might drown," I said.

"Oh no, I know what I'm doing. See that diving board out there? Well there's three tires about twenty feet down, all attached with a chain. Let's see if we can get the tires up."

"Swell," said Neil. "How about you, Little Bob, are you game?"

"Okay, Neil, but let's cut a larger hole in the ice."

It took us some time but we cut a hole four foot in diameter through the one-foot thick ice, and then we took off all of our clothes. Boy, was it cold. Neil went in first, staying down about two minutes, then coming up shivering and wet.

"Say, Neil, are the tires down there?"

"Yeah, Big Bob, but I don't think you can bring them up. Anyway, I've had enough," he said, shaking like a leaf while he got dressed next to the fire.

Big Bob and I got undressed as fast as we could, ran out to the hole in the ice, and dove straight in. I could see Big Bob ahead of me as he reached the tires. We both tried to move them, but they wouldn't budge. We came up for air and then went right back down again. On our third try, Big Bob got his foot caught in the chain, but I finally pulled him loose. Both of us were gasping for air when we reached the surface and crawled out of the hole, and we collapsed and lay on the ice and snow. Finally, we got back to the bonfire where we got dressed. We were so cold we shook for an hour afterwards.

That night Big Bob was sick and I was coughing something terrible, but I managed to stay out of my grandmother's way. I could already taste the kerosene and molasses. The three days had passed rapidly and I said good-bye to my friend, promising to see him in the summer. I told him I wouldn't tell anyone why he got sick.

I was feeling rotten myself with occasional dizzy spells. Arriving home, I was put right to bed and didn't get out for the next three weeks. After about one week, with my cough not getting any better, my dad brought old Doc Whinnery home with him from the city. The doctor said I had pneumonia and he didn't know if I would make it or not. He was against moving me to a hospital, but did make a tent out of a sheet which was kept over my chest and face, with a vaporizer inside to ease my breathing. He left medicines for me to take and told mother when I was to have them. He also told her he thought she should call the priest to give me the Last Rites.

Father Tweeney couldn't come to the house but the next morning a young priest from some other parish arrived at our front door. He came into my bedroom and I told him I wanted to confess and take Communion. He nodded to me and asked my mother to leave the room, which she did. Then he closed the door behind her, knelt down beside my bed, and stuck his head under the tent so that he could hear me. After I confessed my sins, he took a priest's gold traveling cross out of his bag, along with a chalice, set up his little altar on the dresser, and then said the Mass. Just after the consecration of the wine and host, I saw a streak of bright golden light come straight down in front of him and rest on the cross. I sat upright in my bed and the priest stood still as if he were frozen. We both saw the light and were both frightened. The light slowly disappeared straight up through the ceiling of my bedroom. Since we had no electricity in our house at that time, we knew it couldn't be that.

The young priest then gave me Communion and, as he put the chalice back in his case, he took the gold cross, brought it to me, placed it in my hand, and said, "This belongs to you, God bless you." With that, he opened the door and told my mother, who was sitting outside, that I would live. He then said his good-byes and left.

I've never seen that priest since, nor did I ever find out to what church he was assigned. I hid the cross under my pillow, and it wasn't until about three days later that I began to show real improvement and was able to get up. When I showed it to my mother, I told her that the priest had given it to me. I never told her or anyone about what had happened in that bedroom. She was so glad that I was well, and so was I, that I forgot about inquiring after the young priest and in another week I was back at school.

I kept the golden cross on my dresser, and in a few short years it accompanied me to the service and into World War II. It was during the British Solomon Islands campaign, on the island of Guadalcanal, that I lost it. I had unscrewed the cross from its round stand and was carrying it in my pants pocket where it must have fallen out during our trek through the jungles.

During the days and weeks on the island I contracted malaria, which reoccurred three or four times, along with dysentery. I was pretty sick some place in the jungle, but I made my way to our base hospital. There they put me on a stretcher and tagged me for evacuation to the New Hebrides Islands, above five hundred miles southeast of Guadalcanal, where they sent their hopeless cases to die. However, I wasn't ready for that. Instead, I picked myself up from that stretcher, told the corpsman who was yelling at me to lie down to go to hell, and staggered out of that hut.

It was at that time that I reached into my pocket and found my cross was gone. I've often thought I would like some day to go back to search for it, but perhaps someone who needed it more, found it. If so, I hope it brought them hope and peace of mind. I like to think that somehow God gave it to me and, when I no longer needed it, took it away.

20

THE WINE BARRELS

My first year of high school was over and I had gotten through by the skin of my teeth. That year I was going to grandmother's for a couple of weeks right after school. Then I was going to the Altons' farm for the rest of the summer.

Things must have picked up a little because my dad now had an old car and was able to come home each weekend. Sunday afternoon my dad and I left to visit my grandparents in Grand Rapids. Arriving at the house, I said my hellos, put my suitcase upstairs in a bedroom, and went next door to see my friend.

After greeting each other we went outside and started to stroll as we talked. Soon we found ourselves at the Buchanan schoolyard. I learned that my friend had run away from home for a week, earlier in the spring. He had ended up some place in Indiana before being picked up by the cops.

"Bet you had fun, eh, Big Bob?"

"Well, Little Bob, after three or four days of sleeping in old barns, not getting enough to eat, being chased by both dogs and people, and tossed out of a store for stealing bread, I was pretty happy when the cops caught me and called my dad to come and get me. I didn't even whimper when my mother gave it to me good, and boy, did she. I don't think I'll run away again, but I wish I didn't have to go back to school."

"How come, Big Bob?"

"I just don't like school, Little Bob, and I'm always getting into trouble there. I'm going to quit as soon as I'm old enough."

A few days passed, during which time we played with our friends, and Bob's girlfriend was with us just about half the time. Marjorie was some girl, and could do anything we could do, pretty much keeping up with us in everything.

One day, about the middle of the week late in the afternoon, Bob and I were sitting on his front porch when he turned to me and said, "My mom has gone shopping so let's you and I go down in the basement and put on my boxing gloves and spar for a while."

"Fine," I said, and we boxed for an hour or so, neither one of us really hurting the other.

Then Big Bob got a glint in his eye and said, "I have an idea, Little Bob. See those wooden barrels on that side of the basement?"

"Sure, Big Bob, it looks as if they're wine or cider barrels."

"You're right, Little Bob, that's exactly what they are. I bet I can drink more wine than you." He had apparently forgotten what I had told him about my summers at the Altons.

"I don't think you can, Big Bob, but I'll tell you what I'll do. I'll bet you the cost of the show Friday night, and if you win I pay, and if I win you pay."

Big Bob liked that idea. He said, "Get that siphon hose and we'll start drinking the wine right now."

I picked up the rubber hose, pulled the wooden plug out of the top of the barrel, and stuck the hose into it. They were large barrels so there certainly was no chance of being able to drink them dry. They must have held at least fifty to seventy-five gallons of wine each. Big Bob said, "You start first," so I put the hose in my mouth and started to suck up the wine. When I got the wine to my mouth I held it there for about three minutes instead of swallowing it, at the same time keeping enough pressure on the hose so that the wine would stay to the top to further the farce.

"Come on, Little Bob, now it's my turn," said Big Bob, so I handed him the hose.

All the time that I had the hose in my mouth my friend thought I was drinking the wine, but I really wasn't. I would spit some out once in a while, just to make him believe I was really putting it away.

"Okay, Little Bob, it's my turn again," he said.

This went on and on for about forty-five minutes, when all of a sudden Big Bob's face got as red as fire and he vomited all over the floor. Then he began prancing around, and said he was going out to find Neil and the rest of the gang and beat the hell out of everyone. He staggered up the basement stairs, stumbling over everything in sight. When we reached the kitchen, he pushed over the kitchen table with all the luncheon dishes on it, and out the door and down the alley he went.

We couldn't find any of our friends, so instead we went to the old circus grounds along the railroad tracks. There we met a couple of high school boys and got into a fight with them. They were bigger than we were, but we beat them anyway. We fell in the creek as we were trying to cross it, threw a few stones, and just plan raised all kinds of hell. I wasn't drunk but my friend was soused. The effects of the wine hung on and on. It took a lot of talking, but I finally persuaded him into going home. I had to get behind him and push him most of the way to his back door—he wasn't navigating too well.

By the time we reached Bob's house, his dad was home. He took one look at Big Bob and dragged us both into the kitchen where he raised holy hell with us. Big Bob was sassing his dad left and right, when all at once his old man hauled off and let him have it. Bob was out cold. His dad picked him up, threw him over his shoulder, and took him upstairs where he threw him in bed.

My turn was next. Bob's dad came downstairs, grabbed me by the arm, and pushed me down the basement stairs where he handed me an ax and made me chop holes in all of the six barrels of wine. He then grabbed me again and marched me to my grandmother's house. It was a good thing I was going home the next day because I wouldn't have wanted to listen to my grandmother's lecture any longer. Grandad left the room, and I suspect he took a walk around the block, probably laughing like hell.

The next afternoon, before leaving for home, I sneaked next door to say good-bye to my friend. We sat upstairs in his bedroom and laughed our guts out. His house smelled like a brewery.

"No more wine for me, little Bob, but tell me, how did you drink all of that wine and not have it bother you?"

"Well, I guess I'm just a better drinker than you are," I said, "and you owe me the price of a movie show when you get it."

"Okay, Little Bob, have a good summer. I hope we can get together again before the summer is over. Guess I had better stay here in my room today. Everybody's still pretty angry with me. Good-bye my friend, see you soon."

"Good-bye, Big Bob, see you later." I was ready to go back to the farm with my dad. I never did tell Bob how I fooled him by not drinking that wine.

21

SECOND, THIRD, AND
FOURTH YEARS OF HIGH SCHOOL

During my second year of high school one of my friends, Merrill, had an old car, a 1928 Chevrolet sedan. We sure had a lot of fun with it. Merrill sometimes picked me up at home in the morning, or he met me at school where we picked up our other friend, Howie. Then we all went joy-riding, and at the noon hour, we sometimes raced around town, tearing up and down the main street as fast as the car would go. I used to take great delight, when Merrill let me drive, in racing up to a corner, and reaching down and pulling back on the emergency brake so that the car would come to a screeching halt and anyone in the back seat, usually Howie, would come flying forward. We sure had fun screeching tires as we were rounding corners, and sometimes even jumping curbs and working our way back into the street again.

About this time Howie started dating a nice girl by the name of Eloise, and I had my eye on her girlfriend, Marjorie. Over the months Howie and Eloise became inseparable, and for three years, Howie, Eloise, Marjorie and I went just about everywhere together. Howie and Eloise had a peaceful romance, finally marrying a few years later, but Marjorie's and mine was sometimes pretty stormy. I must admit that most of it was my fault.

There were some wonderful moments between Marjorie and myself during those three years. At times our eyes would meet and we would be lost in thoughts of each other, not concerned with anyone or anything else in the world. I thought she was a queen, even though I was quite ornery and gave her a rough time once in a while, but somehow it wasn't meant for us to be together.

I went off to war and Marjorie married someone else.

In the last two years of school I ran on the track team, played football, and took up boxing for the sport of it. Of the three, I really liked boxing. I started training late in the fall in Grand Rapids at one of the larger gymnasiums, and hitched a ride to the city after school each afternoon. After training my dad picked me up and took me home.

Those were the years of Joe Louis, Barney Ross, and Two-Ton Tony. I trained and patterned myself after Joe Louis. I had a fast and straight left hand with a strong right cross. Both of the years that I boxed I was a Golden Gloves champion, and was praised in the following newspaper articles:

Bob Holt, a Coopersville High School boy, knocked Earl Kowal of Caledonia cold in the third round of the bout. A terrific right to the chin put Kowal flat on his back.

Bob Holt advanced in the flyweight division by stopping James Andrews of Lakeview with a hard smash to the chin that dropped Andrews's face flat to the canvas.

To Bob Holt, Gobel Post novice flyweight, went the honor of taking the first title of the evening. Holt outpointed Peter Mackie, a Camp Wolverine CCC lad, who was a willing mixer but who could not cope with Holt's sharp rights. Mackie took an eight count in the first round, but weathered the storm gamely.

The great Arthur Donovan was the ring referee and refereed my fights at the Civic Auditorium. This was no small building, but an arena seating some five to ten thousand people and was pretty much filled to capacity each night during the fights. I had some twelve to fifteen fights there, and in most of them I knocked out my opponents. I decided, after taking a bad beating one year, that I had enough boxing, and I wouldn't turn professional as I had planned. I had fought my last fight.

22

GRADUATION, WORLD WAR II,
AND THE PRESENT

The spring of 1940 was now coming and my friends and I were graduating. Our class had decided for graduation we would take a tour of Chicago.

On our trip to Chicago, we crossed Lake Michigan in a steamship, and spent the day going from place to place. I remember thinking that Chicago was a great city and the hub of our country, and that some day I wanted to come back and possibly make my fortune there.

Some years later, after the war, I did just that. I came to the great sprawling city of Chicago, where I met a wonderful girl from upper Michigan whom I married and with whom I have lived a good life. I have never been disappointed with this great city or with my life.

In the spring of 1941 I was the best man at my friend Big Bob's wedding, and right after that I entered the U.S. Marine Corps. War was being waged in Europe, and, although many times I had predicted to my friends that our country would be in the war before too many months, none of them seemed to be concerned about it. People seemed to have the tendency to look the other way or to shrug off anything that wasn't touching them personally.

It was after spending a few months in the Marine Corps at Quantico, West Virginia, that we received the news that Pearl Harbor had been bombed by Japanese aircraft. Shortly after that, I was given a four-day leave which I spent at home in Grand Rapids. The second day home I met some of my classmates at a beach party arranged by the class. It was good to see them all again. I believe I was the only one in the service at the time and felt it would probably be my last meeting for a while with old friends, for I knew that I would be going overseas with the First Marine Division. I tried to tell some of my friends that night that I would be leaving, but I don't think I ever did. I just couldn't get the words out. Sure enough, a few weeks after I returned to the base, I was sent to the South Pacific.

Now, thirty-five years later, I attended a class reunion. Except for four or five persons, I had seen none of my friends until this reunion. When we met again it was as if all of the years had disappeared, and once more we became young men and women, reliving our school days. How we would have liked to turn back the pages of time!

Some of us have now left this world, including my good and dear friend Big Bob. Though we drifted apart over the years, I never stopped missing him.

I hope I shall continue to live a full and satisfying life with many more exciting happenings waiting around the corner for me. Whatever my future will be, it can only equal, but never surpass, the times spent with my friend Big Bob—we had life, youth, and most important of all—love and friendship.